Spa Wars

Also by Lora Condon

Fuhgeddaboudit Salon and Spa Consultant Kit

Spa Wars

The Ugly Truth about the Beauty Industry

Lora Condon

iUniverse, Inc.
Bloomington

Spa Wars
The Ugly Truth about the Beauty Industry

Copyright © 2011 by Lora Condon

Names have been changed to protect their privacy unless otherwise stated. Even if you think you know whom I'm writing about, you may be wrong since so many product lines or businesses are almost identical. These are my personal opinions, personal life experiences and personal interpretation of them. Please consult your doctor or dermatologist before using any of my favorite products or recommended treatments. They may not be suitable for everyone.

The information, ideas, and suggestions in this book are not intended as a substitute for professional medical advice. Before following any suggestions contained in this book, you should consult your personal physician. Neither the author nor the publisher shall be liable or responsible for any loss or damage allegedly arising as a consequence of your use or application of any information or suggestions in this book.
iUniverse books may be ordered through booksellers or by contacting:

iUniverse
1663 Liberty Drive
Bloomington, IN 47403
www.iuniverse.com
1-800-Authors (1-800-288-4677)

ISBN: 978-1-4502-8591-9 (sc)
ISBN: 978-1-4502-8590-2 (dj)
ISBN: 978-1-4502-8589-6 (ebk)

Library of Congress Control Number: 2011900425
Printed in the United States of America
iUniverse rev. date: 1/10/2011

I told you not to be stupid, you moron. – Ben Stern

All my thanks to God, the Spirit that provides endless love, support and joy.

Kim and Delayne – Thank you for all your support, love and most of all, your money.

Mom and Dave – Thank you for entertaining all my crazy ideas throughout the years.

Jen – aka Yenta. I can't believe I met you in a chat room and here we are! Thanks for all your creative juices, graphic design and man stories.

Tory Johnson – Thank you so much for all your help, support, optimism and loyalty throughout the years. I feel so lucky to learn from you.

Alex – Thank–you for shooting the cover. Only a real friend will bail you out of jail on Thanksgiving.

Thanks of course to all the clients, coworkers, and bosses who made this book possible.

"Beauty's where you find it."
Madonna – Vogue

Contents

How It All Started

If a well–known Haitian voodoo priest tells you that your life has been so interesting, you need to write a book about it, can you really argue with him? I mean, really now! If someone who practices voodoo; tells you that your life is out of the ordinary, can you disagree? Well guess what, in the beginning of 2002, my friend recommended I see a popular voodoo priest for a reading. His reading included the exact details of my past, present and future life. I have to say the past and present at that time were amazingly accurate. He also said that my life had been so crazy, and such a rollercoaster, that I should write a book about it. I wasn't sure how to take this advice. Either my life had been so great or so pathetic. So I went home to start writing and after a few pages, I realized it was the latter of the two. I immediately stopped writing because reliving my life was a bit too depressing, and who really cared anyway? I have friends I can bitch to and I'm sure my friends were pretty fed up hearing about my trials and tribulations. I know I was completely exhausted.

Let's fast forward from that reading in 2002, to mid 2006. I still had the urge to write something, so I started writing a book I planned to title; Just Your Average Angry American. It was supposed to be a book that covered all kinds of topics that pissed off the average person, i.e. ME. Much of the book revolved around politics, stupid people and my crazy stories from working in the spa world. Given the political tension of the time, I thought I was onto something with the title alone, so I started writing like a fiend on the train going back and forth from New York City to D.C. for work. I sent over a segment from the book that pertained mostly to spa stories, to one of my clients who is well versed in literature and what publishers want to read. She told me the spa stuff was what everyone wanted to really hear about and to drop the political stuff. I figured she knew better, so I heeded her advice. As I started telling everyone about the book I was writing, people started asking me about what really goes on in a spa room once the door is closed. They wanted to know what really goes on in the beauty industry. I had no idea people were really fascinated about the intricacies of the beauty industry. Here are just a few of my real life experiences. The book is broken down into four sections. The first section is a compilation of all my stories while working on the beauty industry. The second section uncovers common lies or myths propagated by cosmetic companies, advertisers and magazines. The third section addresses common questions and complaints about beauty issues. It also gives tips and tricks. The fourth section lists all my favorite beauty and health items as well as the best therapists, treatments and organizations.

Spa Wars

Let me start by saying this; I love the beauty industry with all its flaws. It's kind of like a dysfunctional family. It's yours, it's fucked up, and you love it just the same. Of course for your enjoyment, I'm relating most of my horror stories and all the negatives. I have had many, many positive experiences in this industry and thus the reason I continue working with people. I absolutely love it, and this is where much of my heart resides. I love healing people. I love teaching people how to take care of themselves and their loved ones. I love making sure that a teen with acne will learn the proper techniques to take care of their skin, and not make it worse or have scars. I love helping someone learn to love themselves and appreciate their own valuable gifts they bring to the world.

There are plenty of books written about the touchy, feely good stuff going on in a spa, but nothing about the reality of how that is accomplished. In a restaurant, you might sit at a cozy table, with an attentive waiter who was supposed to go home an hour ago. If you go back into the kitchen, people are sliding all over the wet floors, banging into one another, dropping food, burning their hands on hot plates, and people yelling at the cooks to hurry up with their order. The chef is cursing up a storm in English and Spanish, in order to speed up the whole process. It has to look flawless and effortless, once anything or anyone leaves the kitchen door. All you know is that the wine is fine and the food comes on time. You have a great meal, leave a generous tip, and tell your friends all about what a great time you had. This is basically how the spa industry works except there is a little more cursing and just as much food!

1

People are funny: the ones I have worked for and the ones I have worked on. One of my favorite lines from clients is, "This must be the most relaxing job ever!" I would say, "Honey, I'm not the one getting the massage!" They would always look at me and say, "Oh yeah, I guess you're right." I'm happy that I can make people feel so good, that they think everyone else feels good. Hopefully, this book will give you a clear understanding of what really goes on, in order to give you five minutes or five hours of spa and salon services. I'm about to give you all the spa–tacular details of the beauty industry. This book includes my experiences from day–spas, cosmetic counters and freelancing as a makeup artist.

For over ten years I worked in the spa industry as an esthetician. For those of you who don't know, that's someone who does facials, waxing, makeup and other treatments in a spa or salon. Most of the places I worked catered to a high–end clientele. Celeb's, ladies who lunch and other various scum with a black Amex who think you should jerk them off for a bigger tip or any tip at all. Many times, the richer they are, the cheaper they are. The one exception tends to be white men in business suits. They almost always tip well. My most generous (and most appreciated) tips come from blue collar, or blue–collar moral people. They respect someone who is hard working and actually appreciate the fact that I make my living trying to make them feel better mentally, physically and even spiritually. I have nothing against the rich, trust me. I want to be one of them. I just don't understand how someone becomes so oblivious to everyone else around them because they have money. Ok, enough preaching and lets get this story started.

My Life's Work. Mistake Or Destiny?

I guess I'll start from the beginning of how I ended up in this crazy industry. I was working on my master's degree in drug and alcohol counseling, at night; therefore I needed a full time day job. I got a job as the admissions counselor for a cosmetology school in New Jersey. The school was run down, and had not been renovated in at least fifteen years. I should have known then, but ignorance is bliss, I guess. At that point, I never had a massage or facial. I'm not sure if I even had a pedicure. I'm sure I must have had a manicure, but I honestly don't remember ever getting one before working at this school. I soon learned, cosmetology schools only teach students what the state board requires them to teach in order to pass the test. They only teach the bare basics. It's just like certain public schools, where they teach you to only pass the basic skills test. Ultimately, the students became disillusioned and angry at the lack of education provided. The teachers were so beaten down, that they no longer tried to teach new techniques for fear of rocking the boat. It's a shame, because there are many talented teachers and students that are never allowed to "be all they can be."

One day, while working at the cosmetology school, the esthetics teacher needed a model so the students could practice doing a facial. I was dying to get a facial and see what the heck I was selling! At this time, I had no idea what really went on during a facial. That day I entered the dark facial classroom. It smelled so good and the dim lighting set the mood. I put on a robe and got under the sheets. As the student esthetician put her hands on my face to start cleansing, the heavens opened up, and I suddenly knew my destiny. Finally, in my mid twenties, I had a vision for my life. How could it have taken me this long? By mid facial, I think I was snoring and dreaming of putting my hands on anyone who would stand still long enough. I wasn't allowed to attend the same school I was working in, so I started my search for another school in order to attend night classes for esthetics. Since the esthetics license was so new, I had to wait around a few months for a school to start a night class. I obviously chose the only other school that had night classes at that time.

To get a hint into my past, I was groomed to go to college, work at the same job forever, get married, have kids and retire. My mom had her heart set on me becoming a lawyer working 9–5, pushing papers, and pretending to like safe office work. My mom always said, "You can do anything you set your mind to. There are all different types of law!" To think about becoming an esthetician, which most people can't even say, was close to blasphemy. To have a safe backup, I found a completely horrific job in the billing department of a law firm and that's about as close as I would get to ever becoming a lawyer. This job was during the day and it paid every Friday. Perfect. I went to work Monday through Friday until 5pm and then Monday through Thursday I drove 50 minutes to school (assuming there was no accident on the parkway).

School started at 6pm and ended at 10pm. I then drove home about 50 minutes. I did this for 10 months straight. When I told everyone what I was doing, they thought I was completely insane.

This particular school sells you on the hope of assisting in the owner's spa, then finally working there. It sounded good to me. I haven't even started and already I am assisting. I was so excited on the first night of class, and then I learned that my teacher never even gave a facial. In fact, she never worked in a spa as an esthetician. She took a mini–update class at another esthetic school, and was now qualified to be a teacher? I think we had around 6 girls in the class. There was never a full class, so I can never remember how many students actually enrolled. My teacher thought that because she wore MAC make–up and went to a dermatologist, she was an esthetician. She didn't even know how to pronounce major skin conditions. She called rosacea – ROSA–sia. She taught us full time until the end of our training. The revolving door of teachers was unbelievable. The products we used for learning were far from sufficient. Queen Helene, Mint Julep Mask can only take a girl so far in New York.

One of our many next part time teachers was a young girl. She was great and actually worked in a salon, which helped us with practical, applied knowledge. She eventually quit teaching because the school was so bad. It was great to have someone teach us, who actually worked in a spa and could tell us what was going on in the real world. We then had another teacher who was completely amazing. She had a huge medical esthetic practice in New Jersey and actually taught plastic surgeons about areola restoration. So for me, she was close to God, and everything I wanted to become. She taught us the real way things were supposed to be done. I gave her a facial once, and she told me I had butterfly fingers. It was then, that I got the feeling that I might be on to something, and I made the right decision to become an esthetician.

Unfortunately, this teacher didn't last more than a month. One night during class, someone from the corporate office called her out of the room. They told her that they wanted us to reuse the rubber gloves for extractions, and to only teach us what was in the book. They told her not to teach us anything advanced. This was totally unreasonable because while doing extractions, one is supposed to wear rubber gloves because of blood, pus and other contagious goo that comes out of the pores. According to the Board of Health and general common sense sanitary regulations, when you're done with the extractions, you throw the gloves in the garbage. That is unless you go to the school I went to, where the owner actually told us, and the teachers to reuse the gloves. How disgusting, not to mention illegal. I can't imagine the Board of Health telling us to try and sanitize bloody gloves. Obviously, this great teacher was aghast when she heard this, walked out, and never returned. I guess she never saw *Norma Rae*! She quit, and I went back to my misery of making hundreds of cotton pads for facials, which my old teachers considered learning.

Our next teacher was this old, fat woman, who would sit at the desk and snore while we practiced on each other. On one of the rare nights where she was awake watching me give a fellow student a back facial, she leaned over, looked at my friends back and said, "Oh my God, that's a boil on her back!" I leaned over and said, "That's a pimple." She proceeded to argue that it was a boil but it was just a small typical back pimple. The student I was giving the back facial to started freaking out, thinking she had a boil on her back. We laughed about this for months. We had no choice, but to go to the corporate office and tell them that the teacher was falling asleep in class and knew nothing. She didn't even know how to use a steamer. That was the last night we ever saw that teacher.

Many nights we just hung out in the manicuring room talking and bitching about how much money we paid for school and what we actually got for it. Most nights my boyfriend came and hung out with us. He actually had a better attendance record than most of the students. One crazy Moroccan girl rarely showed up, and when she did, she was coked up. All she talked about was her men and how they would buy her anything she wanted, including her boobs. She was the typical hot, crazy bitch that men couldn't wait to get abused by and abuse them she did. She never finished taking the class as far as I know.

One other girl in our class quit before the halfway point, and transferred to another esthetic school. We started with five or six girls and only two or three actually finished the class. I think I'm the only one who ever went to work in the field though. We were halfway through our class, when they started the second night class. There was no teacher on their first night of class. We told the girls all our horror stories about the school and how many nights there is no teacher. Every single girl immediately quit and we never saw them again. Word got to the owner and he was livid. We were so proud of ourselves. It was not the first or the last of my "Norma Rae" moments, as my mom would call them. Deep down, I knew some of the teachers thought it was great. We said and did what they couldn't, without losing their job. It took me years to learn how to keep my mouth shut, and I guess in writing this book, I still have a lot to learn. I just can't take injustice no matter what the situation. I especially can't take the BIG corporate machine taking advantage of the unsuspecting honest "regular Joe." At the end of my schooling, I wrote a letter to the owner, but for some reason he never responded. Maybe he was too busy washing bloody gloves.

The First Job

I attended esthetic school at night and worked during the day in the law firm. Friday night and Saturday morning I worked as the receptionist in a salon and day spa. This is probably the worst and hardest job in the salon or spa. The receptionist is the person that everyone complains to about anything and everything. The receptionist gets blamed for wrong appointments, lost money and tips, unhappy clients, clients that are lost in the salon, someone not getting coffee fast enough, or having someone on hold too long. The list goes on and on. Receptionists are the most abused people in a salon and spa. From a receptionist's point of view, here are a few annoying things NOT to do:

1. Don't call the last minute for an appointment and keep asking if the receptionist is sure there aren't any available appointments. The receptionist is not lying to you when they say "No! There are no openings." People think they are the only person calling for an appointment for 10am, Saturday morning. These are probably the same people who get off an escalator, stop at the bottom, and think about which direction they want to go in. Yes, I am the person behind you that pushes you, and makes the decision for you!

2. Don't call a salon without a backup date and time if your first choice is taken. If your first choice is taken, don't take

another 10 minutes to figure out what other day you might want. This is when the receptionist puts you on hold so you can figure it out, and goes back to the 3 other lines with people trying to figure out when they want their appointment.

3. Don't ask to speak to the stylist so they can squeeze you in. This is so obnoxious and makes you look like you think you're important. If you were really that important, they would cancel someone else, and that only happens for beauty editors and celebrities. The goal of a spa or salon is to take clients in order to make money. There is no reason someone would not book you, unless you are not welcomed at that establishment.

4. Don't expect your spa person to do something you wouldn't do. Don't expect them to stay late at their job and not take a lunch, if you wouldn't do the same. Sometimes we will stay for clients who tip very well or if we really need the money. I have to admit, I have also stayed late for hot, single men.

I'll Have a Bloody Bikini, Waxed Not Shaved

"The pain passes, but the beauty remains." – Pierre August Renoir

Halfway through school, I got my permit to work in a salon. I stopped working reception, and got a job working Saturdays at a salon in a ritzy north Jersey town. The owner was a Turkish woman, who was a bit crazy, with big frizzy brown hair. At this point, in the history of my beloved New Jersey, big frizzy hair was no longer "in" at least above exit 130 on the Parkway. She was about 5'3 only clearing 5'0 without the hair. She was a little chubby and always wore black spandex pants with a tight animal print shirt. This salon also had a little punk rock girl who cut hair and one older gay guy. One gay man a salon does not make. I don't remember how I got paid, but it was probably just 30% straight commission on services. Here, I discovered I was a pretty good sales person, because I sold $30 cleansers like hot cakes. The facial room was an old boiler room. It had pipes going up the wall and all. There was no door to the facial room, just a curtain as a door and a curtain covering a cutout in the wall that opened out into the salon. You basically got a facial with all the noise of a hair salon. But hey, people went for it and I needed experience.

This salon is where I had one of my scariest experiences ever, my first bikini wax. I knew I was great at facials. Waxing was not my forte the first year or so. I was never really even taught how to do an eyebrow the right way until 2006, when I worked for Anastasia of Beverly Hills, the eyebrow guru! I'll never forget that first bikini wax. She was a young, Spanish girl with the coarsest hair I have ever seen. With each pull, blood appeared out of every pore. I was petrified. I had no idea if this was right, or if I was pulverizing this girl's bikini line. Let me apologize to this girl now; I'm so sorry that you were subjected to being my very first bikini wax. Maybe it was your karma. If that's the case, well hey, karma can be a bloody bitch. Looking back, it is common for some blood to come out of the hair follicle when waxing. I don't think I did anything wrong, but I'm not sure. That is why I highly recommend getting referrals from friends, coworkers, and family, before you trust someone with your privates! It is not always the big name on a spa that means anything. It's totally the technician. The bigger spas don't always have good technicians. Big spas usually employ technicians with no experience, because all of their money goes into advertising, decor and public relations firms. This was also the salon where I did my first full leg wax. I used more than half a can of wax and the owner flipped. Keep in mind, a can is only $10 and she knew it was my first job. It can be easy to go through half to a third of a can for a full leg wax on a larger woman. I worked at this salon until I finished school, and then moved on.

Crack Is Whack

Yes its true, crack is whack! I worked in a high—end mall in New Jersey that the diva herself used to frequent. There are two classic stories that were told to me via co—workers. Unfortunately, I missed both episodes, so I can only quote what I was told. One time, Ms. Whitney came into one of the cosmetic stores to shop with her daughter. That's normal right? Well it would have, had she not been acting high, and wearing more than one shoe. Yes, someone let Whitney "out da house" only wearing one shoe. She was yelling at the staff to "put lip gloss on my baby," meaning her daughter. She was also yelling around the store, "where's my huuuuuusband at?" The second shopping episode was quite similar, but that time she was shoeless. You know why no one is accusing me of being a crack head? It's because I don't go near the shit. That story reminded me of Mayor Marion Barry in DC. No one will ever find me hitting the pipe in a hotel room, unless something goes really, really wrong in my life. If her voice weren't totally destroyed from all the smoking, she would have had a great comeback. Get back to Jesus girl, and please don't ever do another reality show about how great your marriage is working. Marriage reality shows are the kiss of death, in case you haven't noticed.

Impeach Bush

Cooch etiquette! Open a Playboy magazine and make it your Bible! This is more important than Vogue, Cosmo or any other magazine that won't be as explicit. By explicit, I don't mean sexually. I'm talking about cleanliness. If Vogue shows us how we should look on the outside, than Playboy shows us what should be going on underneath that Gucci. Playboy women are a lot meatier than Vogue anyway. Yeah for Playboy! It's ironic how people criticize Playboy for exploiting women but Playmates actually eat. Every time I watch the *Girls Next Door* show, all they do is drink and eat. They just balance it with working out and bangin' Heff. Many fashion models barely eat or exercise. Unless you consider exercise the contractions their stomach makes while they force themselves to puke up veggies and diet coke. It's kind of like reverse crunches.

Let's get back to the cooch. Modern American grooming standards dictate that Playboy vagina is basically how a vagina should look. It should have little to no hair, so cut that damn bush for God's sake. This is one time when I would actually agree with the saying, "IMPEACH BUSH." If I were a man, I would be very afraid to go down on some women over forty. They seem to have been left out of the whole vagina grooming revolution. That's why that scene in the movie Scary Movie, where he takes her pants down, and an afro comes out of her underwear, is so funny to me. I swear that's pretty close to reality. I'm always surprised when a woman comes in for a bikini wax with a huge bush. Those clients usually come in and want me to wax the hair that comes out from the sides of their granny pants. I try to get them to let me wax more, but they don't seem to mind the goo filled tangled mess. When I tell some women they have to cut the hair so it doesn't stick out from the sides of their bathing suit, they look at me like I told them where the Arc of the Covenant was hidden. And it may very well be. How could someone not figure this out after 40 years of hair sticking out from her bikini bottom? Did Annette Funicello know this? Maybe her stylist was ahead of his time and knew the importance of pube grooming even back then. Just think of Marilyn Monroe's dress blowing up, and a big tangled bush sticking out from her underwear.

Sorry, but the whole hairy, unkempt vagina grosses me out. Let's not even discuss a big hairy vagina with a pad during your period. Can anything get grosser than that? Tampons, ladies if you can. So in conclusion, wax or shave your bush into a Brazilian. That means remove all the hair off your vaginal lips, and ass (Yes, there is a lot of hair in your ass crack. After all, crack is whack.), and take a pair of scissors and cut the hair down to almost nothing in the front. You can leave what I like to call a "Hitler stash" or as some call it a "landing strip." Any basic shape is fine as long as it's cut close to the skin.

On a serious note, it really cuts down on smell. I don't think I need to explain why, but since we've gone this far I might as well. As far as I know, all women have vaginal discharge. If there is a lot of hair on the vaginal lips, that discharge penetrates the hair shaft and ferments all day long. If you urinate, guess what happens. Excrement is also another big problem if you have any anal hair. That bacterium sits in your anus and vaginal area all day long. If you don't shower extremely well at night before sleeping, that is another potential 8 hours of bacteria fermenting. This is one of the main reasons women are instructed to never wipe from back to front after a bowel movement. Under a microscope, hair strands have overlapping jagged, scale–like edges. It is very easy for fecal matter, urine and discharge to get stuck in all the nooks and crannies of each hair. Thus, the more hair, the more bacteria will remain and cause potential problems. With no hair, it is very easy to wipe after going to the bathroom. If you really want to do it right, use a baby wipe or something of the sort to keep the area especially clean. You'll be amazed how much cleaner you get when wiping with something wet after a bowel movement. People always wonder what we're thinking about while we're waxing someone's bikini. Well, we're thinking about lunch! We're thinking about what we want to eat, where to get it and if we have made enough in tips to eat sushi for lunch. I know it's gross but it's so true. Most of spa life revolves around food.

You Go Girl, Whatever Your Name Is!

My first full time job was for Adrien Arpel in Bloomingdales. There were two rooms behind the counter in the back corner of the cosmetic department. I loved this job and I loved my boss. Unfortunately, by the time I got there, Adrien sold the company, and it was in financial turmoil. The job went like this. Do an hour facial and a make–up application, sell and close the sale, clean the room and get the next client started, all within an hour. This is where I learned to hustle and do a really fast, great makeup. I learned that as long as you give someone a great facial massage, they don't mind if the facial is a bit short. I wasn't trying to jip them, but I only had an hour to do all that stuff! Everyone loved my facials and since we were pretty busy, I got better fast.

Here's some background on the Adrien Arpel Company, as it was relayed to me from the then current employees. Let me state for the record that this is the story that I was told from the people working for the company at that time. I do not know the truth. This is just was I was told. The person everyone knows as Adrien Arpel is just the face of Adrien Arpel. Her name is something like Irma Rothstein from Lawn–Guyland. When she left the company, she left it in financial disarray and started Signature Club A on Home Shopping Network. The AA company was supposedly suing "Adrien" for being called Adrien Arpel on Home Shopping, and using that name and image to sell her new products. I think she sold the Adrien Arpel name along with the company. The HSN products were extremely similar to the original Adrien Arpel products. I don't know Adriens side of the story of why she is not involved with the original company, but I'm sure it would make a great book. Knowing corporate people, she was probably right and the suits were wrong. Looking at her financial success now, she got the last laugh!

The HSN products were so close in name that people would come to the counter all the time and ask for whatever cream she was selling that week. We would show them a cream with a very similar name and no one ever noticed the difference. I didn't feel bad doing this, because I needed the sales. I also felt the original products were better and much more effective. People were always trying to return the HSN products. Then we had to tell them that the Signature Club A products had nothing to do with the Adrien Arpel products. People got really pissed! They just assumed because it was the same person that it was the same products, even though the names and packaging were completely different.

An interesting thing happened after about five months of working for Adrien. I realized I was getting paid the same amount of money as my boss. I thought this was disgusting, but a really good lesson in how to stand up for yourself or no one else will. I personally believe she had a victim mentality, where she subconsciously didn't believe she was worth more. SO NO ONE PAID HER MORE! She was working there about 11 years and I got paid the same amount walking in the door. Eventually she found out, and I felt guilty, but not enough to give her the difference. About eight months later, we started receiving jumbled shipments of products. We started getting old cosmetic bags and old products that were dried up. You could tell they were sitting in the warehouse for years collecting dust. This could only mean one thing. I'm now on the Titanic and I have to decide if I want to jump or go down with the ship. I chose to jump. A few months later, my boss was suddenly laid off. She was surprised, but I couldn't see how she didn't see this coming for a while now. I think she just loved her job and the company so much, she never thought of leaving on her own. I loved Arpel's original products. I could watch Adrien or whatever her name is, all day long.

The Big Bad Spa World

I seem to get jobs that teach me something I need to learn. It's not even about the job; it's about what I have to learn while I'm there, to get me to the next level. Since there is really no such thing as loyalty anymore between employers and employees, I just assume that I will only be at a job, as long as it takes me to learn what I need to know, and then I'll move on. I know this may fly in the face of traditional business, but it seemed to work for me. I can't say I've gone about this career the most secure way, but it definitely has been the most adventurous.

One of my first interviews while looking for a new job after Adrien was at this beautifully renovated salon with a new spa added. The owner had an extremely loyal clientele, and his staff followed him all over New Jersey. It was your typical hair salon with young beautiful people doing hair. Of course the other side of this was drugs, drinking, random coworker sex, cheating and bitch fests! Ten–hour days in stilettos and very tight, designer clothes can do that to a girl. There was one hot guy there who was a dark version of Fabio, just not as humble as Fabio. They were hip, hot and fucking nuts. I went into the interview and did a facial on the owner. His wife, who also did facials, watched me. He had fallen asleep, snoring and all. They were remodeling the whole place to be French Victorian or French Country; something frilly and expensive. I'm not really sure of the difference between the two, but it was very oh la la!

The interview went well, but then I didn't hear from them for a week. I called the spa and the voice message said the owner died, and the spa would reopen in a week. A few weeks later, I started working there. This is where I learned all about the insanity of salons. I soon learned there was a ton of bad blood and bad history with this salon. It was the typical story of how once the leader is gone everything falls apart. There was another part time esthetician, who sold her own makeup. I think I got paid about $400 a week and when I doubled that in services, I would get 30% commission. Not bad for a nice spa. The trick was to be busy.

Priorities being what they are; one of the first things the wife did after her husband died, was go out and get herself a new pair of tits. For the first few weeks, she spent everyday holding her boobs and complaining how much they hurt. I kept wondering why she wasn't holding her heart considering her husband just died. They had a ten–year–old son together, and he was the spitting image of the dead husband. It was very scary to look at him since they both had very captivating eyes. A few months after I was hired, they had the grand re–opening party. It was definitely bitter sweet, since the owner had just died and this was his vision. In grand fashion, almost every stylist got wasted and started fighting at the party. Somehow I ended up in a dark massage room with a bunch of the old staff. It started out with nice conversation and nice memories of the owner. As more people came in the room, it ended up with everyone screaming about old affairs, back stabbing and other indiscretions. I quickly slid off the table and exited the dark room, so as not to become a part of the new stories. It seemed that just "being there," somehow made you a part of the drama and I was sure I would eventually I get dragged into taking sides. This salon was a reality show before they existed.

Dirty Laundry

The salon had only one washer and dryer for laundry. This was a big problem. You can't wash spa towels in the hair washer and dryer because all the hair will get in the spa towels and that's pretty gross. I would put our used spa towels, sheets, and robes in big plastic bags for the owner to put in her Boxster. All she had to do was drive it home to her cleaning lady, and bring it back the next day, simple enough. The first two times it worked out great. Then the bags just seemed to sit in her office and she wouldn't take them home. Everyday I would tell her the laundry needed to get cleaned anyway possible, because we had no more clean linens left. So what did I have to do you wonder? Yes, folks, I had to open up the dirty laundry and reuse it on clients. That was so disgusting, that I had to start telling other staff members, in the hopes that someone could get this woman to care about something other than her boobs. Let me remind you, these were wet towels with creams, oils and other unknown substances on them, tied up in plastic garbage bags. Clients paid $80 to wear a robe and headband that had been used for the past two months by almost every other client. The sheets, yes, those were laid on by every other client for months. Yummy! Eventually, she had to throw out the laundry bags since they turned an interesting shade of gangrene. No wonder my coworkers stopped getting facials. This is some stuff you just can't make up.

Full Disclosure

One day right after a client filled out paperwork for her facial; the Fabio guy came back to the spa and started walking towards me. This was strange considering he barely even breathed in my direction. He came up to me and whispered, "I just wanted to let you know that your client has AIDS in case she didn't tell you." I immediately looked at her medical form she just filled out, and there was no mention of AIDS, illness or medications she might have been taking. The first time Fabio actually spoke to me, he told me the client I'm about to squeeze pus and bodily fluids out of has AIDS. So I got my "new" rubber gloves for the treatment and proceeded to throw them out after the facial. I should have mailed them to my old esthetic school as a donation, and maybe I could have written it off on my taxes.

I know a lot of salons and spas do not do intake forms. This is really dangerous. You never know what is walking in the door and what they have. It's very important to protect yourself as well as the client. They might not realize that it's dangerous to wax if they're on insulin. They may not realize that doing too many peels can damage the skin. You cannot make every client tell the truth, so it is very important to get as much information as possible. Every client should sign a form giving his or her medical history. If they sue you for taking their skin off, at least you can protect yourself by saying that they never stated they were on Retin–A, even after you asked them!

After working there a few months, the other part time esthetician left to work full time at her other spa job. Since the makeup was hers, she took it when she left. For about a month, the owner knew the esthetician was leaving, and she also knew she was taking the makeup with her. I had make–up appointments scheduled and everyday I reminded the owner that we needed to get makeup so I could do the appointments. She brushed me off in usual fashion, as if I had no idea how to run a business. I now understand why her husband sometimes locked her out of the salon during work hours! I was only there a few months and the negligence was unbelievable. A few appointments came and went, some were rescheduled, and some were pissed off. I bet the owner could have just brought in her own makeup and I could have done the makeup appointments. Eventually, she ordered make–up for the spa.

The layout of the salon was such that the spa was all the way in the back and no one even knew the salon had a spa! So I suggested that the make–up be put in the front, where it can sell itself, with a sign about spa services to attract customers. Again, my suggestion was met with disdain. I was happy to get the make–up, but they never ordered a make–up stand. I ended up doing make–up from make–up that was lovingly placed on the floor. Yes, on the floor. Clients paid $75 for a make–up application from the floor. This is disgusting and unacceptable. I had to tell the staff again, what was going on in order to protect myself. I also hoped that the older staff members would talk to the owner, and help her to get her act together. At that point, I was looking for any way to make the spa more efficient, so mentioning this to coworkers was a last resort. At least put it on a snack tray bitch! Eventually, they did put the make–up on a professional stand in front of the salon to attract clients.

Shitty Pants Club

BIG update for women – Don't buy a new Louis Vuitton bag, get a manicure or read one more Cosmo, until you buy NEW UNDERWEAR! With all the sales that Victoria's Secret has, I wonder who is actually buying all this cute underwear. Maybe the secret is that women don't really wear that stuff. They just keep it in the drawer for special occasions. Well honey, going to see your waxer is a special occasion! I see your cooch and undergarments in the bright, white light. Men usually see you in the dark and don't have time to inspect your thong. Women have this thing where they save their crappy (pun intended) underwear and wear those when they have their period, so the nice ones don't get dirty. Ok fine! I'm a girl; I get that and have a few crappy pairs of underwear myself. For the love of GOD, don't ever wear those on a day where someone other than your cat might actually see them!

99% of women are clean, normal and get waxed with no drama. However, that 1% is what makes this profession memorable and book worthy. Sometimes, I feel like the Statue of Liberty. Give me your tired, poor, stinky, stained underwear. The crunchy, torn masses yearning to be free! Throw out any underwear that has shit, blood and yellow discharge stains. I'm completely embarrassed for, and ashamed of women who are nasty in this area. Guys always think it's so hot that I wax vagina. I tell them the truth of how dirty some women can be, and that I'll never be a lesbian from this experience. I'll take stinky balls any day! Bring on the beer farts. One lady smelled so bad of stale urine in her long, uncut pubic hair, that I couldn't finish waxing her bikini. I actually told her, I didn't have enough time to do all the waxing she wanted. She was upset I didn't finish, and came back the next day to have someone finish her waxing. My boss (who was also a proud member of the shitty pants club) finished waxing her crusty cooch. It was only fitting that my boss suffered, since she would make me wax her own pissy, smelly, cooch. Sometimes there is not enough commission in the world to do that!

Twice the Clients, Half the Tips

"You think that's a confrontational tone? Then you know, you should really see me when I'm pissed." – *New Jersey Governor Chris Christie*

So now with more experience and lots of positive feedback from clients, I felt armed and ready to go to a bigger and more exclusive "real" place! In the late 1990's, I started working in a spa in North Jersey. It was a small place, but in an exclusive area and very busy. The only semi–glitch was that I had to do two facials at the same time. Let's say the first facial started at 12pm. I would start that facial by cleansing, steaming, extractions, massage, and then a mask. At 12:30, I would go to the next room and start cleansing and steaming the 2nd client. They would steam while I went back to the first room and removed the mask and finished the client. Then I would go back to the 2nd room and do extractions and massage, then put the mask on. While their mask was on, I would go to the first room and start a new client. Repeat the process for 8 hours!

This way of doing facials is not the norm, and really cheats the client out of an effective facial. As long as I gave them an amazing massage, no one complained that they were left to steam for approximately 8 minutes. No one should ever steam that long. You just end up making them red and dehydrated. A major problem occurred if someone was 5 minutes late. We would have to work that much faster or lose the tip, facial and potential product sale.

The benefit of doing two clients at once is that the spa makes twice the money, twice the product sales, and they can fit in twice the amount of clients. We made twice the commission on services, and twice the commission on sales. If someone didn't show up or cancelled their appointment, it didn't really matter to us or ruin our day. There is a big difference in losing a half hour appointment, opposed to a full hour appointment. Here's a bit of advice for people who go and get services done by the same person on a monthly or semi–regular basis. If you tip us well, we will really take care of you, and you will get preferential treatment. We will squeeze you in, give you better service, give you gifts, etc. If you don't tip 15–20%, you can forget getting an appointment before Christmas or New Years. You'll get the appointment when we know we're slow and just need a warm body in the seat. I know this sounds horrible, but so is not tipping. I treat you how you treat me! Would you go to the same restaurant all the time and not tip the waiter? No, of course not. All the waiter does is bring you your food. They don't even cook it or touch you!

I had one client give me a $10 tip on her first facial. I was happy because I was warned about how demanding she was from the manager. She sung my praises to the manager and the manager was happy. The next time she came in, I gave her a great facial thinking I would get the same tip. When she left the room, I noticed there was only $5 on the bed. Hmm, was the facial bad or was she just low on cash? So I let it go, but wrote it down in her chart. With all my clients, I would write down how much the person tipped me on every visit. In reality, this determined the facial you got! The 3rd time she came in, I gave her yet another great facial, to the tune of a $5 tip. So I figured the extra $5 from the first time was my Christmas present. Then I started to give her the $5 facial. The $5 facial meant a massage with a very light touch. Everyone wants a firm massage. Every time I give a firm massage, my hands have that much less life and longevity in them. Since I make my living using my hands, I'm not going to waste my moneymakers on a $5 tip. She eventually told the manager that I wasn't giving her great facials anymore, and specifically the massage part. The manager opened the chart, saw the tip history, and knew the exact reason why there was a change in the facial. I made no bones about my policy with my boss.

You respect me and I'll respect you. Maybe it's the Jersey Italian in me, but that's how it goes.

One time a girl came in for a facial and told us how sensitive her skin was. She said that everything made her break out and get rashes. So why the fuck are you here douche bag? I mean really. It's like people set you up, for you to make them break out in hives with their negative self, fulfilling prophesy. I did her facial with all the same products I use on everyone else. Of course she came back the next day broken out in hives. She complained to the manager and the manager looked at the inside of her chart, and BAM, there it was; a big fat 0 in the tip column. The manager knew it had to be karma! Don't mess with Lora and her money! I can't make someone break out or get hives, but karma can be a bitch.

We had another client who was a cheap accountant. Now you would imagine an accountant would know how much to tip. She came every month and would give me $3 and the makeup artist $2. At the same time, she would always show off her huge diamond engagement ring, so I knew this was no student or poor person. One day I went up to the make–up artist while she was doing the accountants makeup, and handed her $20. I told her it was from her last make–up client. We used to do this in front of the clients who were shitty tippers to hopefully jolt them into realizing their $2 tip is a waste of our time. Again, we ended up getting $5 between the two of us! People like this are just so oblivious to everything else in the world that doesn't revolve around them.

This spa was run very well. The owner basically stayed out of the spa and let the manager do her thing. We had a manager who always did the ordering and laundry. The products were stocked, retail was available and it was smooth running. Here was the only problem for me, and the eventual reason I ended up leaving. We sold tons of gift certificates and packages without the tips included. Ok, fine, that's what spa's do. That's really how spas stay alive. Kind of like a gym. The business makes the money whether you show up or not. Of course we like to have clients everyday, but the owner gets the money, and they forget about how important it is to have the client redeem those gift certificates to keep the business alive and growing. Retail is the real moneymaker for salons and spas. It's also what puts the business over the top in terms of revenue and profit. This is usually why estheticians hound you to purchase products. Many times the clients that come in for facials need better or more effective products. They don't really sell for the 10% commission as much as the owner or manager constantly yelling at them to sell more products. Retail makes the spa money, while the workers are not seeing a client. Retail is king and might be the only reason someone comes into the salon or spa. That is the reason why I choose to only work at places that have products I love to use and sell.

The overwhelming majority of people, who buy gift certificates, don't include the tip for the recipient. This is the equivalent giving the gift without the batteries, except these batteries can cost anywhere between $5–75 in tips depending on the cost of the services. If a facial is approximately $80, the tip should be about $16. Most people getting the service never asked for the gift certificate, and now they are not going to tip on a gift they never asked for! I can't blame them, but at the same time, don't get a service and not tip. Just buy products with the gift certificate from the spa if you can't or won't tip. With the amount of gift certificates we sold, this was starting to become a major problem in my daily income. Why should I work so hard and continue with severe carpal tunnel for no tips. Traditionally, gift certificate and package clients are usually not serious clients. They are there to get away from the kids for an hour, or just use up the gift that was given to them a year ago. They don't usually upgrade their facial; buy products for homecare or tip! This started to become a real annoyance and loss of income on my end.

To remedy this problem, I suggested that we should include gratuity in the package price. At least 15%, just so we get something. I was met with an emphatic NO! I knew this would be the answer, because I had been complaining for a long time and nothing was done. People looked at the bottom line price of the package, tip included or not. People then bought the cheapest package because of sticker shock with tips included. From a business standpoint, you could say it was smart for her to say, "No". On the other hand, it was not smart, because the spa workers need incentive. The manager at this time told me my attitude was becoming bad and it better change or else I can find another job in two weeks. She basically told me that I was on probation or something. I told her that I'm pretty sure my attitude wouldn't change, unless the tip situation changed. She told me that the tip situation wouldn't change, and we left it at that. I figured that was my two weeks notice. When the two weeks were up, and I told her I wasn't coming back, and she flipped. I was like, "umm excuse me, did I miss something here?" I was under the impression that we decided on two weeks and then I would leave! Oops, silly me. On a side note, after I left the spa, the manager added the tips to the packages! I just take it as God pushing me into another field of work and God teaching me a few lessons.

There was a makeup artist who also worked at this spa. She was an ex–model, who did make–up for Playboy magazine at one time. I would watch her work on clients and examine her end result. I never really saw her do a makeup that I felt I couldn't duplicate. This somehow gave me the bright idea of being a makeup artist in some kind of freelancing capacity. I had no idea what that industry was like or what it entailed, but I just had a feeling that I needed to find out. I started to take classes in New York City on Mondays, which was my day off. In those classes, I learned all types of make–up. Working the hours I did at the spa, left me no time for freelancing. The seed of success was planted, and there was nothing more I ever wanted, then to be successful in New York. New York means so much to me and it's so much more than a city. It's a friend, a teacher, your enemy and destiny all rolled into one! Go Jay-Z!

Meeting Micky

While I was freelancing, I decided to take a part time job in a spa to supplement my income. I started working in an existing spa, where a woman with a lot of money bought the spa and remodeled it. She hired a spa manager we'll call Micky, to help her with managing and daily operations. The owner still had her own ideas and the final say on all decisions. Again I learned that just because someone has money, doesn't mean they know how to run a business. Just because they might be successful running one business they know a lot about, doesn't mean they are going to be successful in running another business they know nothing about. In true womanly owner fashion, she had tons of retail and not too many clients!

The facial rooms were upstairs in a very old house that was kind of creaky. The rooms were large colonial style. Normally when doing a facial, the esthetician sits at one end of the bed, with the client lying down on their back, with their head close to the end of the bed where the esthetician is sitting. This is obviously done so the esthetician can easily reach the face of the client without moving. The products are always at arms length, at the side of the esthetician on a roller cart or countertop. This is done so they can be reached without making noise or disrupting the flow of the facial. Not here! The owner wanted the treatment products put on an armoire. Ok fine. She also wanted the armoire on the other side of the room. So every time I wanted a new product, I had to get up and walk across the creaky floor and get it off the shelf. I explained to her how abnormal this was, and how it would totally interrupt with the quiet relaxing flow of a facial. She said she didn't care, because she thought it was pretty to have the products perfectly lined up on the armoire on the other side of the room. Ok, sleeping with the enemy, whatever you say!

A few days later, we had a staff meeting and another employee questioned the owner about another one of her crazy ideas. The owner gave her a stupid explanation that basically equated to the answer my mother would give me when I was a kid; "because I said so, that's why." Of course I opened my mouth and said something like, "Don't bother asking her, she's not going to change her mind anyway." The next day Micky fired me. While she was firing me, she said she felt really bad, because she knew I was right and that the owner was a bit crazy. It would be the first of many lessons I needed to learn on keeping my mouth shut when confronted with stupidity. I just don't think I have the capacity to not voice my opinion. I swear I'm trying though, really I am. Micky told me that I was too good for that spa and she would try to get me another job with her connections. I didn't believe her, but figured I would try to salvage whatever I could at that point. The manager told me the house was haunted and she heard voices and sounds at night. I would soon learn they were probably the voices in her head! Eventually, Micky and I did work together again, and I realized that God blessed me once by getting me away from her. The second time I worked for her, I'd be on my own in getting away from her!

New Yawk, New Yawk

"Now we understand much more clearly why people from all over the world would want to come to New York and to America. It's called Freedom." – *Rudy Giuliani*

Off I went to the big bad city to see if I was as good an esthetician as I thought. At the time, I was starting to build my makeup portfolio. Most of my tests and shoots were not paid or paid very little. The paid work was few and far between, so again I decided to get a part time job in a spa. The interview process can be long and difficult. Many spas look great from the outside, and then they are a completely different story when you work there. They usually don't have health benefits, steady clients, or the owners are not good business people. Many times, the pay is low or commission only. You never really know what you are getting into until you are working there. Sometimes, you just hope for the best. Most spa owners are very aware that it's a fleeting business, and they are usually the reason for job turnover. They are always trying to find a way, to not give someone the money they've earned. Many are horrible at managing people. Bait and switch is a technique that spa and salon owners use frequently. It could be with products, clients, services and pay. Many times owners put cheap products into the expensive bottles and the clients never know. This is common with the shampoo used to wash your hair. They'll use any available products for your treatment if the one's they're supposed to use are out of stock or the name brand is too expensive to keep buying after the initial purchase. One time I had to mix cuticle oil and grocery store brown sugar together for an expensive body scrub. On a whim, the owner can switch clients from one therapist to another and many times the client will accept it since they're already at the salon and want the service.

Some owners will hire someone if they are the right astrological sign! YES, I was offered a job because I am a Capricorn. Apparently, this was a sign the owner approved working with. That woman still has a salon and spa in New York. She has a few people who have worked for her for years, and then a revolving door of victims who can't deal with her unprofessionalism. Some people will deal with the insanity if they can make money. I can deal for a bit, but I have my limits. Years after that interview, I became one of her spa consultants. I couldn't get any estheticians in New York to work for her because of her crazy reputation. For months after re–opening her spa in a new location in New York City, she couldn't get herself together enough to have an opening party. She also made the foolish mistake of opening a salon in the Hamptons. Apparently, she didn't realize that the business in the Hamptons is seasonal which forced her to close down.

Stink Fist

After sending out tons of resumes to salons and spas, I got a call from Bliss Spa, a huge spa in New York City. At the time, there were only one or two locations. The call consisted of a man on the other end asking me about twenty to thirty questions regarding the skin, protocols, and other basic esthetic questions. If you passed that test, you came in and gave him a facial. I passed the phone test, and I went in to give him a facial. I passed his facial test and then I was scheduled to go back again to give Marcia Kilgore, the owner of Bliss, a facial. I thought this would be my big break. This was the one place I really wanted to work in New York. I was so excited to actually meet and work on Marcia. She is a huge success story and someone I would love to emulate in many ways. I think about her ability to go from doing facials in her apartment, to creating Bliss. She is a business genius and marketing mogul. I'm not sure how she is to work for, but she was very gracious at the interview. Her skin was really great even though she thought it was bad. Typical girl. She had that glow. She was the real deal. I think she had connections with models to get start–up money and big clients but I'm not sure. At least she was smart enough to take advantage of it and keep it going and growing!

At the interview, I was confident, but nervous as hell. This was the big time! I was overly nervous to work on her, which is not like me at all. When I went in the room, the interviewee before me was on her way out and she was very pretty and well put together. While the girl was leaving, Marcia mentioned that she would contact her for the next step in the interview process. Marcia and I got started; she started asking me all kinds of skin and technical questions. She then asked me if I liked to cook. I was surprised and thought maybe she was asking because she thought people who liked to cook made better estheticians. I mean at this point, no question from an owner would surprise me. I said I liked to cook, and she asked if I cooked last night with garlic. "Yes", I said, and she said, "I know, I can smell it on your fingers." BOOM! That sealed my doom. I knew at that point my shot at Bliss was over, and I might as well have left right then and there.

A few days later, I called back and asked the first man I spoke with, why I didn't get the job. He said Marcia's notes stated that my hands were too strong. I figured she meant the pressure, but I know she meant the smell! Although I was really sad over not getting this job, I do believe that everything happens for a reason. Had I gotten this job at Bliss, I never would have been able to do the freelancing makeup gigs. Marcia, "Can I get a redo on that facial?" Anytime, it would be my honor to work on you! You make me proud to be in this industry in terms of business sense, marketing and starting from square one.

Completely Cheap

After many interviews, I ended up working in another very well known spa in New York. I thought I hit the mother load here. This was a popular spa, with monthly magazine mentions and lots of celebrities. There were two locations and I worked at both of them. One of the estheticians was mostly booked with her established clientele of laser and waxing. The second esthetician didn't do Brazilians, so she did facials and laser. Depending on the staff on certain days, that would leave me getting stuck doing almost eight hours a day of Brazilians! I think I waxed half the cooch this side of the Mississippi. Brazilian waxing was not my specialty at the time like it is now, and certainly wasn't my favorite spa service. Laser was new and interesting, and the wave of the future for spas. Laser hair removal was not really emotionally gratifying like facials. Great, I zapped your hair, but I always felt like the "hands on" was what really renewed people. It felt like a car wash, clinical and clean.

There were a few problems working here. The owners were completely cheap. Here I was at one of the most popular salons in the country, and they only paid $9 an hour. No commission on services and I don't recall earning commission on products. If we did, it was no more than

10%, which is not an incentive. What I do remember is one of the estheticians sold about $10,000 in laser services to one client and they didn't even buy her a cup of coffee! Talk about cheap! I actually got mad and thought that there was no way I could continue working for people who did not reward their employees. When I took this job, I thought I would get really big tips based on the price of the services. I ended up getting little to no tips doing laser, because people see it as a medical service.

One day, I was supposed to wax a female celebrity by–product. That's basically an unknown person, who is only famous for dating a celebrity. Not long after their break–up that male celebrity got married. Apparently, the ex–girlfriend and current wife frequented the same salon. This day they were booked to be in the salon at the same time. So what does any respectable owner do? Cancel the ex–girlfriend and take the wife. That's the difference between the A–list and any other list. The owner called the ex–girlfriend and said there was a mix up in booking, and rescheduled her. I was really pissed because the wife was a client of the other esthetician. I didn't get to do the celebrity; I didn't get the tip and didn't get to fill her spot on such short notice. The celebrity's wife also had a tab at the spa that she didn't pay. I couldn't wait to see her, because it was a big deal at the time in New York City that this particular celebrity dumped the girlfriend and suddenly married this woman. She was so tacky and frumpy, I couldn't believe it. The ex–girlfriend was very fashionable and pretty, so I was expecting the same from the wife. The wife showed up in jeans tapered at the ankle with a bedazzled denim jacket and gold lame flat shoes. She was tacky, tacky lawn–guyland. And people *tawk* about New Jersey? She was a real *miserab'* as we say in Italian. She might be very nice, but I didn't see it that day.

This spa was run very well and organized. The only thing was that no one liked one of the owners. She was a very cold person. I don't know if she was nice or not, but that's the way she came off. The other girls knew her better than I did, and I know they didn't particularly care for her. To this day, that salon is a revolving door of employees. I laugh to myself every time I see a posting for a job there. Most of New York has done their time there. I have all the respect in the world for the owners though, in terms of business. Well, except for the cheapness.

She was extremely responsible in making sure no one worked on a client unless they were 100% solid in their skills. I have so much respect for this, since most spa owners don't take into consideration the skills of someone. I have worked for owners who never had the person do a facial before hiring them. That's like hiring a typist and not having them take a typing test. Most owners hire someone based on the way they look or their gut instinct. This is one of the reasons most spas and salons fail within a year or never reach the top.

One of the owners was male and we all swore one of the estheticians was in love with him! She would swear she wasn't, but she would show a lot of cleavage and kept trying to get a promotion. He was that typical successful, good–looking, New York stockbroker type, who was completely emotionally unavailable at forty years old. He dumped every nice, sweet girl that he brought into his web of deceit. I wouldn't doubt it if he was considered one of the most eligible bachelors forever! There are a lot of broken hearts strewn along the Long Island Expressway en-route to the Hamptons. Funny how that long and winding road is called the L.I.E.! I think that's what you get, when you finally get to the end of it!

After working at this spa for a while, my freelance makeup jobs started to pick up to the point where I couldn't work both jobs. This was one of the scariest points of my life. It really is like jumping off a cliff. Freedom has a price, as we know. The price of freelancing is no health benefits, no set income, and you could go months with no money coming in. Come to think of it, freedom is friggen crazy, and that is why most people take the nine to five routes. They also happen to be in a constant state of misery. Is a bird with clipped wings in a cage that never flies, still a bird? We love the bird for its song and grace in movement, yet we keep it in a cage. Sounds similar to what we do to ourselves. Some of us choose to fly and take the risk. I chose to leave the KuKu's nest and started to freelance full time.

Hairy Lip

How could I forget about lip waxing! Just do it. Don't bleach the caterpillar on your lip. There is nothing sexy about a blonde caterpillar, caked in makeup above your lip. Just think about your lip gloss running into your mustache! Come on ladies. If your esthetician asks you if you need your lip waxed, that means you do. It's like if someone asks you if you want a mint! Duh, take it Chewbacca! If you are of a certain ethnicity that is prone to dark or any lip hair, just wax it, and welcome to America! Don't forget the bikini area, shitty pants!

Freelancing, A Remnant of the Roman Empire

"Coercion after all, merely captures man. Freedom captivates him."
– *Ronald Regan*

The term freelancer goes back to the Roman Empire. It's a military term. Smaller states would have leaders that were supported by "condottiere," who would fight for the leader. A "condotta" was the contract between the condottiere and his temporary master. It was a guarantee of his loyalty or good conduct. The condottiere, were organized into groups of three called, "lances." The lance consisted of a mounted soldier, his squire and a lancer, either on foot or mounted. Since these soldiers were mercenaries, loyalties shifted frequently like politicians. If the opposing side offered more money or other accolades, the lances would often change sides. The lancers, who frequently changed commanders and sides, became known as "freelancers." It's not so much about not being loyal, or keeping your word, as much as it is, who values me the most by paying me the most.

Freelancing, no matter what industry, is not for the faint of heart. If you decide to freelance, be prepared to learn more about yourself and others than you ever dreamed possible. You will live for your phone and email. You'll be up at 3am, looking online for jobs and networking. It's amazing how a lack of money will force you to talk to people and promote yourself, when you'd rather sleep, eat, disappear, rest, go out with friends or any other activity that doesn't advance your career. The idea of working a room, getting each other's business cards and schmoozing is great, but I absolutely HATE doing it. It's kind of like socialism; great on paper, horrible in reality.

Eventually, your family and friends will come to understand that even if you say you're coming for Christmas dinner, if a job comes up, they can wait till next Christmas to see you. These are the things you do to be successful. That one job you don't take will be the one job that catapults your replacements career. I constantly read about the lives of successful people. Not one of them played video games, watched TV, or shopped, over work. They are all focused like rain man, on the goal at hand. I'm pretty laid back, so I have to force myself to go the extra mile sometimes. Here are a few of my crazy freelance stories. I have had less insanity while freelancing makeup than working in salons. I tried to figure out why, but I haven't been able to yet. Maybe since freelancing is short term, you're not always privy to people's insanity on short notice. Maybe going to the same place everyday makes you crazy. If you ever consider freelancing, think of pressing on until your goal is met, to the exclusion of everything else that may stand in your way. That was very much the mentality of the Roman Empire.

Dude, I Need a Hit

"I don't need Michael Moore to tell me about September 11th."
– *Rudy Giuliani*

Like most starving artists, I got a p/t job as a waitress. This is a job reserved for saints only. Nothing will make you hate people more, than serving them food. I tried to do this job, which was completely horrific. At the end of a shift, you were supposed to get checked out by the section leader and make sure your section was clean and not one more sugar packet could fit into the sugar holder. I swear, I thought I would lose my mind when they told me I couldn't leave until there was no more room in each sugar holder for one more packet! They actually checked. Many nights I successfully ducked the sugar Nazi. The restaurant business can be a big scam. They pay you $5 an hour, and make you stay all night in case a rush comes. What rush? The gold rush? It usually never comes, and of course I always tried to sneak out before the end of any late night shift.

Early one morning, I was listening to Howard Stern and he was talking about how a plane went into one of the twin towers. He automatically knew it was terrorists and even mentioned Osama Bin Laden was probably responsible. Looking back, I think Howard Stern should be taken more seriously. His gut instinct is almost always right on target. Of course, I thought Howard was joking so I turned on the news and sure enough, he was right. The world was never the same. I wasn't going to go to work that morning but my boyfriend at the time told me I was weak and stupid if I didn't go to work, so I went. On top of the events for the day, the credit card machines were down, half the staff didn't show up, and we were bombarded with people sitting, watching TV and getting drunk. At the time, all I had to do was take a five–minute ride to Rt. 3 in Secaucus and watch the smoke from the pit change colors. Obviously, it was a horrible day and it took me three hours to get home when it should have only taken me ten minutes. I was stuck behind a white truck that was supposedly filled with explosives. Thank God it wasn't.

The next day, I was at the restaurant again, and I got a phone call from an art director from a magazine. This was the same person that months before, I wrote a random 3am email, asking if he needed a makeup artist for any photo shoots. He said his regular makeup artist wouldn't come back into New York City, because she was scared and he asked if I was available for a shoot the next day. Hell yeah I was available! Who did he think I was, some weak Jersey girl? It was a major publication, and I was so excited. He also asked me if I knew any male models to bring to the shoot. I made a phone call to the hottest model I knew, and he met me at the studio.

The next day I drove into the city, and it was eerie. It was a ghost town on many different levels. I'll never forget the feelings of a quiet New York on a weekday morning. It was the first time I actually wished for traffic going into the city. With traffic, the drive into the city took me about and hour and 15 minutes. That day, it took me 15 minutes. Going into the Lincoln Tunnel was completely freaky. You drive the whole ramp going in towards the towers. This day, all I could see was smoke at the tip of New York. It was one of those trips where I don't remember thinking about driving. I don't remember taking out the money to pay the toll. I don't remember breaking or accelerating along the ramp. I only remember smoke. Smoke changing colors. I knew that each smoke color meant something else was happening down there. They were digging up new fires, falling debris, and smoking remains. As I drove along the streets, I saw firemen walking all covered in ash, and fire trucks from all over the country driving through the streets headed south. I don't remember looking at the streets for directions, or arriving at my destination. This made me wonder if I was doing the right thing. Was this what being strong was? Was I so poor and weak that I took a job to make some money, capitalizing on someone else's weakness? Maybe that's America, and I was just being a good American. Capitalism is in my blood. Maybe that's what it was all about; moving on, in spite of. Not going back to normal. I hate that saying. There was nothing normal about this. Nothing has been normal since that day, and the world is forever changed. I also find it disgusting that the mosque will be built at Ground Zero before a memorial.

We were shooting the Xmas edition of a magazine dedicated to pot! Hey, beggars couldn't be choosers at that point. The female model happened to be someone I worked on before at an event for Steven Van Zant, at the Hardrock in New York. My male model friend came and completed the eye candy. It was strange to work given the obsession with one topic over the past days. There were actually one to two minute spans of time during the shoot that I didn't think about the attacks. I felt incredibly guilty for each of those moments at the end of the day. How selfish could I actually be? At the end, they divvied up the props and lit them. In the beginning, I didn't think it was real pot. Boy was I surprised when they started smoking it! I'm not a drug person, and I don't even like being drunk. I don't like to be out of control of my body. The sound of my mother's voice in my head stops me from overindulging. But, given the circumstances, it was exactly what I needed. I was about to have a nervous breakdown from despair, sadness and tangible anger. As we left the shoot, we were given some pot to take home. I never even smoked it. I gave it to someone else, whose nerves where just as shot as mine.

We said our goodbyes, and I made my way back to my car and back through the tunnel in my drug haze! Driving through the Lincoln tunnel high was a surreal experience. Surprisingly, that was the first and last time I ever did that. Everything had a yellow buzzing overcast, with blue florescent lights, like a time warp taking me back to September 10, 2001. That dream was shattered when I exited the tunnel and didn't see the towers. I thought, "Am I so friggen high, that I went through the Holland Tunnel instead of the Lincoln?" I kept driving, and finally realized that I didn't see the towers exiting the tunnel, because they were no longer there. It was strange, because I honestly don't ever remember seeing the towers there before that day. They were a subconscious thing that was always there, and your brain just accepted the fact; every day since I notice their absence.

Ballerina Bun Bitch

Early in my freelancing career, a mentor recommended me for a popular Turkish TV drama show. I think it was a type of soap opera. All the actors flew to New York and worked with a Turkish–American production company. The shoot was for one week and paid about $100 per day. My boyfriend at the time, warned me to not work with Turkish people. I had no idea why, although I did think of the Turkish salon owner in Jersey, who was a bit strange. I assured him I could get along with anyone to further my career. I got to the hotel room Monday morning, at 5am, to start the first day of hair and makeup on two actresses. I did the hair and makeup for the first actress, and it went well. I started the second actress's hair, and they told me through an interpreter, that she wanted the ballerina bun that she had from the pre–party the night before. Since I worked on the principle of the New York Ballet, I was well versed in the typical ballerina bun. The hair is pulled back tightly, and wrapped into a bun at the back of the head – very clean, sleek and tight. Have you ever seen a ballerina with messy hair?

While I was working, she started talking to the other actress while pointing at her hair. Then the other actress told me that the girl doesn't want her hair so tight. She wants the bun to be a little looser. I complied. Then she started fussing and talking louder in Turkish. Again, the other actress explained to me that she didn't like the bun and wanted it looser, like it was the night before. I never saw the bun from the night before, but most ballerina buns are all the same. Again, I made it looser. The third time, she got up, took her hair out and did it herself. "This is what she wants," said the English speaking actress. "Oh", I say, "She wants a messy bun, not a ballerina bun." "NO", she wants a ballerina bun." Something was getting lost in translation. Messy bun and ballerina bun never appear in the same sentence, unless we're doing an editorial Vogue version of a coked up ballerina, who finally passes out from starvation. I gave the bitch her messy ballerina bun and got started on her makeup.

I finished her makeup, which they said they wanted to be very natural for the first scene. The scene was friends going to lunch at a Turkish café in New York. While I was putting on the finishing touches, a clearly hung over woman stumbled in the door. I then learned she was the clothing stylist and two hours late. She was also friends with the director, Turkish and didn't shower or wash her face from the night before. The stylist was obviously full of drama, and I could only imagine what the day would hold.

When I was done with their hair and makeup, we got into the car to go to the location where we were shooting. We unloaded into the restaurant, and I started touch ups. The stylist came over and started telling me how to do their makeup. I reminded her that it's natural daytime makeup for a lunch scene. The actresses were wearing jeans and a turtleneck sweater, so I wouldn't necessarily do glamour makeup. She turned around, opened her purse and started to apply a white foundation stick to the actresses face. She added dark blush, big glossy lips and black eyeliner. Now I was really starting to doubt my ability. That never happened before, so I wasn't sure what was so wrong with the makeup I applied. The stylist proceeded to put this heavy white makeup under their eyes. I let her do it, while I assessed the lighting that the guys put up. I noticed they used huge fluorescent lights, like ones you would find in Yankee Stadium. Everyone under the lights looks totally blown out and goth. This white makeup is making them look like the bride of Dracula, and all I can do is sit back, and watch her totally take over. She kept telling me that I didn't know what I was doing and they needed to have natural makeup. I guess in Turkey, white skin and dark makeup on the rest of the face is natural lunchtime makeup.

I told the Assistant Director what happened and how unprofessional this was. She reassured me that it will be ok, and she would talk to the stylist. At this point, half the shoot at the restaurant was over and I just tried to make the best of it. I knew they were talking about me, right in front of me, in Turkish. The assistant director was sympathetic, like she knew this was going to happen. The actress wanted one thing, the stylist another and the director another. I can't do three different makeup applications on the same person, at the same time! We started to shoot, and the director looked at me like I was a complete idiot, because the makeup was so dark. I lightened it a bit, and took the heat. Or maybe it was the stadium lighting. End of day one!

The next morning, the ballerina bun girl told me she wanted long, flowing curls in her hair. Ok, here we go, I thought. I finished her hair and makeup in the morning, knowing we wouldn't shoot her till the afternoon. I also knew that we were going to be on location with no electricity since this was low budget filming. That meant, no re–curling the hair. We shot in Manhattan for a few hours, and then jumped in the car to shoot under the Brooklyn Bridge. As we got in the car to go to Brooklyn, I noticed that the actress who was not with me, since I did her hair that morning, had a coat on, with her hair flattened under the coat, and a thick scarf wrapped around her neck, complete with a knit hat pulled down to her ears! So much for bouncy flowing curls. I had to do her touchups in the car as we drove through the city, because we only had a few minutes to shoot. There was not too much I could do with that flattened hair. Again, the stylist redid all the makeup I had applied to the girls. I just let her do the makeup because at this point, I figured I might as well get paid, and let her take the heat. I couldn't figure out how and why this was happening. I'm sure by now you can see; I'm not one to be a push over or a weak personality. At the same time, I was really confused as how to handle this situation because my mentor recommended me for the job. I didn't want to disappoint her and I didn't want to look stupid. I never had this happen before, so I wasn't too sure what was going on and how to handle it. If I got this job on my own, I would have been more vocal. Obviously, natural makeup means something very different in Turkey.

We finally got out of the car, and shot under the bridge. Again, the director, as well as the actress, was upset with the hair. They asked me why her hair wasn't curly. Maybe because the dumbass put a wool coat over the curls for the past four hours and then strangled the curls with a scarf. It was so windy out, that her hair ended up looking decent. It was shot under natural lighting, yet the stylist used that same white foundation stick. Please tell me you're finding some humor in this story! We finished shooting the scene and went back to Manhattan for lunch.

At lunch, I was freaking out inside, because I knew I couldn't continue the rest of the week with the stylist redoing all of my work. Why even bother having me there? At the same time, I was devastated at the thought of disappointing or embarrassing my mentor. Finally, enough was enough. After lunch, we started to prepare for the next scene, and again the stylist, started to touch them up. At this point, I approached the assistant director, told her the situation and that I could no longer work on this set and I was going to leave. "Apparently, my services are not wanted or needed, and if the stylist is going to do the makeup, then you don't need me," I said. She kept asking me to stay, and she promised that they did want and need me, and that she would talk with the stylist. I reassured her that the stylist was not going to refrain from doing their makeup, and I didn't want to be in the middle between the director, stylist and actress. I couldn't take four more days of this drama. I gathered my things, got in my car, and headed back to Jersey. I reluctantly called my mentor and told her what happened. She said, "Wow, I'm surprised you lasted that long. They were crazy, and the assistant director kept trying to get the makeup done for free." I was so relieved that she wasn't mad at me for leaving. If I had known, it was ok to quit, I would have left the first day at lunch. I was so grateful to get the job, but I couldn't take it. End of story, they did get their makeup artist for free, because they never paid me for the work I completed.

Rat Bastards

There is a store in New York called Yellow Rat Bastard, and the photo department head called on me to do makeup for a shoot in Webster Hall after he received another one of my three a.m. emails. They were supposed to give me a gift certificate for $150 to the store as payment for my services. I would rather have money, but it was free shopping and tear sheets for a cool store. We got to Webster Hall, and I found out I had an assistant because there were so many models. Great! As I talked to her, I found out she only did wedding makeup and had no experience with models, photo shoots or photography makeup. It also turned out that she knew someone who put the shoot together, and that was how she ended up on set. I know that's life, but I work so hard for every crumb and people who have no talent, or work ethic, get jobs based on connections. *That* is the reality of life.

She did all the male models, and I gave her one female model. The female model hated her makeup that the assistant did, but I had no time to redo it. It ended up being a pretty cool shoot. The magazine printed it so dark, you couldn't see ½ my makeup. There is nothing worse than knowing you did great makeup, and it can't be seen. At the end of the shoot, they told us they would send us the gift certificates. It has been more than five years, and I'm still waiting for that gift certificate. I called them so many times, and no one would take my calls, return emails or acknowledge that they didn't pay me what they promised. I was stupid for not getting it in writing, but so many deals in this industry are done on a handshake, it wasn't out of the ordinary to believe they would keep their end of the deal. They really are Rat Bastards!

I'm Like So Not L.A., Ok

One day I was looking online at other makeup artists' websites. I found one girl in Los Angeles who did incredible work, and I sent her an email saying I'm a brand new makeup artist, and that I loved her inspiring work. I also said, if she ever came to New York, I would love to meet her and show her around. I never thought anything of it, until one day I got an email from her saying that she was coming to New York to do an event for a big film coming out. She said she needed help body painting the models, and asked if I wanted to do the job with her and actually get paid. She also asked me to find another person to help us. I jumped at the chance to see how someone of that caliber worked. It was an amazing opportunity, especially since I was so very new.

She arrived in New York, and we met the day before the event to talk. She told me that her airbrush compressor was smashed during the flight, and didn't work. She was freaking out, because she needed to get a compressor by 10am the next morning. I told her that I would call my friend and see if she could lend her one of her compressors. The makeup artist looked at me like I was crazy. I asked her why she was so shocked that I would do this, and she said that something like this would never happen in Los Angeles. I wasn't following her at all. "Something like what," I said. She said that in Los Angeles, the word would spread that you had no compressor, and all the other makeup artists would call the producer to try and take the job from you. "I guess that's why I'll never leave New York," I thought to myself. I called the other makeup artist I knew, and we went to her studio to borrow the compressor. It turned out they knew of each other's work, and I could tell there was some drama going on beneath the surface between the two of them.

The next day I arrived at the event location to start helping her body paint and assist. I told her before, that I just started doing makeup, so I was obviously not proficient with an airbrush. So of course she started me off airbrushing their outfits. At first, I tilted the airbrush and some of the paint spilled out. I wanted to die on the spot, and she gave me the look of death. I felt like a five year old kid. I'm a pretty adventurous person, willing to try anything, so I made the best of it, and tried to make it work. In the meantime, I was still waiting for the other makeup artist I secured to show up and help.

An hour went by, so I called the other artist. She picked up the phone and I asked her where she was. She said, "It's at 10 o'clock right?" I replied, "Yes, and we've already started and we're waiting for you." "Oh, I thought you meant 10pm, not 10am." I should have known not to expect a stripper to be on time, especially at 10am. When she did arrive, she came in heels, daisy dukes, a handkerchief blouse and braided ponytails. It almost looked like a Halloween costume. As she walked in, we all just looked at her and collectively thought, "Are you for real?" At that point, we were painting our little hearts out, and another pair of hands was much needed.

After a while, the L.A. makeup artist walked over to me and said "Put this girl's hair up in a bun." Ahhh, another bun! At this point in my career, I had very little experience with hair and I didn't bring any hair products. As far as I knew, we were only doing makeup. I have no idea how I did it, but I found a rubber band on the floor and a pin that another model brought, and I put this girls hair up. Later, the artist came to me and said, "I just wanted to see if you could do it and test you, to see if you could think on your feet." At that point, I wanted to show her just what I could do with my feet! I found her a free compressor at the last minute, I found two extra people to help her paint all the models, and now she wants to test my hair skills? I was beginning to wonder if no one in Los Angeles would help her because they were shallow back–stabbing people, or was she just crazy and manipulative. We finished painting the people, the event finished, and everyone looked amazing. At the end of the night, she started talking shit about the woman from whom we borrowed the compressor. Apparently, she thought my friend stole her ideas for a body painting project she was supposed to do. I have no idea what transpired between the two of them, but I sure as hell wasn't going to get in the middle or take sides. We were shocked that she would talk about our friend right in front of us.

I tried to change the subject; she complied, and then proceeded to tell us about the drama she was involved in with her last film. She started telling us that she was fooling around with one of the other crew members, and it was the talk of the set. She was telling us this gossip like we were her BFF's! She then started telling us details of her relationship with this crew member, and how they kept denying they were having a sexual relationship. I had no idea what to do, and I just kept trying to change the subject again and again, to something more positive and to get away from the drama. After she tired of telling us all of her Hollywood gossip, she thanked us for being such a big help and gave us some left over products.

The next day, I talked to my friend who lent us the compressor. She said that the artist from L.A. was complaining that I was too slow and not aggressive enough. She said I asked her what to do next, instead of just knowing what to do, and doing it. I was fuming inside, but I kept my mouth shut and took the criticism. I clearly told this artist from Los Angeles, that I was brand new, and had very little experience. This was the biggest job I had worked on at this point. Of course I was going to ask what she wanted me to do, to make sure I was doing the right thing. If I had more experience, I would have taken more initiative, but that this point in my career, that would have been a big mistake. Maybe she forgot that I never really did hair before, and maybe she forgot that I never airbrushed before on clothes or people. I was doing makeup for a few months, and she had been working for about fifteen years doing hair and makeup. I never told my friend that this girl was talking smack about her. I figured that I would cut my losses, and stay out of the gossip and stick with New Yorkers who just tell you that you suck to your face! That was also the last makeup artist I ever wrote to!

Rusty Trombone Anyone?

One day I got a call from a makeup artist who said she found my card in her purse. She needed a makeup artist to replace her on a job, and wanted to know if I was available. She warned me that this was a really crazy shoot, and a lot of the crew had quit due to the insanity. I asked if they were Turkish, and she assured me they weren't, so I said, "Yes." The director was John Herzfeld, and I was excited to work with, and meet him. It was a reality type show for TV, with New York super cop Bill Stanton. He was put in different situations, where he told you how to protect yourself, or your children. It was post 9/11, so everyone was in this "how do I protect myself" mode. The show was actually really good. It was like *Survivor Man*, but in the real world with everyday circumstances.

On the first day, I could see why half the crew quit. It was unorganized, and the director and star were basically having cockfights the whole day. It was like putting the two most insecure men in the world in a boxing ring together. It was really all in good fun, so I found it quite humorous. I was getting paid to watch the show! It was like being a fly on the wall of how men really behave. I think I was the only girl besides the line director on the shoot. I really liked everyone, and this was the type of insanity that I liked; just crazy, ADD artists, having fun, doing what they love. Unorganized, yes. Unprofessional, yes. Fun, hell yeah! Howard Stern and Diceman are two of my favorite comedians, so I was far from offended on this job. I'd work with either one of them again in a heartbeat. I'm kind of a guy's girl, so I like potty humor.

One day we were shooting in the Reebok club, and they spent half the time comparing speed bag skills and the other half checking out the hot girls in spandex. It was kind of silly because Bill is twice the size of John. Later that day, we shot in a cigar store. Bill was friends with the owner, and I thought the owner was totally hot. I told Bill, I was hot for his friend, knowing full well that Bill would tell him as soon as we went back on set. I spent most of that day, talking to a girl who happened to be the owner's girlfriend. The owner was definitely checking me out; once his friend told him I thought he was hot. It was a bit uncomfortable, but he had these eyes that put me in a haze. At the end of the shoot, the owner gave me a bunch of cigars for free. He also gave me his business card with his phone number and a wink. Hmm, what's a girl to do? I never called. I didn't want to be *that* makeup artist.

The next day, I walked in the director's hotel room, and he was freaking out because he burned the tip of his nose trying to light a cigar the night before! I had visions of these guys trying to outdo each other lighting cigars as if they were in the Rat Pack. He actually had a small hole at the tip of his nose the other makeup artist and I had to cover with makeup for the next few days. In the meantime, the only reason he was on camera was to give his opinions and bust balls. He wasn't in the actual show! I think the real show was him, burning a hole in his nose. I wish Bill did a segment on that! I had a good time on this shoot and ended up doing makeup on a former Ms. America, Chuck Zito, and Joey Fatone. I was very happy to be working with good people and getting some good names. Most of the time, I was very quiet in the presence of Bill and John. I really just liked watching them interact. It was kind of like watching the gorillas at the Bronx Zoo.

Towards the end of the shoot, we were all in a van going to shoot some stuff in Times Square at night. I'm not sure how it came up, but I mentioned something about a rusty trombone. John turned around and asked me what the heck a rusty trombone was. We all started laughing hysterical, and shocked that he didn't know what a rusty trombone was. Since he was unaware, I explained to him the intricacies of a rusty trombone. He just looked at me and said, "You said nothing this whole entire week, and the first thing you say is rusty trombone?" I said, "Well, you and Bill are so busy having cock fights that I can never get a word in edgewise." He must have started visualizing how a rusty trombone would actually go down. No pun intended! We had a really good laugh. He was just more surprised that everyone knew what it was but him. Once we got on location, he made me go on camera in the middle of Times Square and describe a rusty trombone. This is what I love about entertainment people. If we were in an office, someone would have been sued for sexual harassment or fired for political incorrectness.

I was really sad when this shoot ended. I really didn't care about the cockfighting. It was like a live psychology experiment. The reality part of this show was the crew, not the actors.

Suzy Chap Stick

One day John Herzfeld called Danny Aiello. This was a blast from the past for me because I met Danny when I was a kid, and I have wanted to talk to him about that meeting ever since. When I was about 10, I used to work back stage at a fashion shows. I helped the models take their clothes on and off during the show. At one particular show, Suzy Chap Stick was one of the models, and from what I remember, she was a bitch. Everyone loved Suzy back then, so I was even more upset to have a bad experience with her. I don't remember what she did anymore, but she made me cry. I think Suzy was just treating me like a piece of crap kid that was under her feet. I was one hell of a tough kid, so I can't imagine what she did to make me cry.

After the show, everyone was drinking at tables that were lined up along the runway. My mom made me go up to Danny Aiello to meet him. I had no idea who he was, but I figured he was someone important, since my mom kept pushing me to go over to where he was sitting. In typical kid fashion, I told Danny that Suzy was nasty and made me cry. All the guys at the table laughed. Then Danny put me up on his lap for about a half an hour, while he continued to talk to his buddies. I was so happy that he was nice to me, and treated me like a person, not a stupid kid. Later on that night, Suzy gave me a totally fake apology, but I was over her, and found a new fab friend in Danny Aiello! Paesanos stick together I guess. When John Herzfeld called Danny, I begged to talk to him. Unfortunately, Danny was in a meeting, and couldn't talk to me or John. I just wanted to thank Danny for being so nice and treating a kid like a person. Whatever you need Danny; I got your back, Jersey style!

Powder Girl

I love Judith Regan, regardless of the troubles she has had in the recent past. She published Howard Stern's book and if she's good enough for him, she's good enough for me! I was scheduled to do her makeup for camera, in her office. We set up to shoot in the conference room, and as I was gathering my makeup she said, "Where's the powder girl? Oh, powder girl, are you the one going to do my makeup?" Eww, are you kidding me? Calling the makeup artist the powder girl, is like calling a flight attendant a waitress. I really wanted to dump my powder on her and play into the bimbo role she assigned me. I understand that Judith has to be one hell of a tough woman to make it in the publishing world, but don't take it out on your fellow women! I've actually done makeup on rappers and gang–bangers who addressed me with more respect. I doubt she meant anything by it, but it's slightly impossible for me to believe a woman of her intellectual status, would not know that she should call me a makeup artist instead of a powder girl. I still love her, and I would have loved for her to publish this book.

Retail Hell

"Lasciate ogne speranza, voi ch'intrate" – *Dante Alighieri*

Working part time at the cosmetic counter was enough for me to get some free makeup, and not have the hopelessness of full time retail. Personally, I believe a full time cosmetic counter job is a horrible job, because retail just sucks ass. Retail makeup is a slow death of creativity and spirit. I figured I could only do this part time, and if I ever thought different, this job solidified that belief. Every time I walked into work, I felt like I was walking under the gates of Dante's Inferno. Lasciate ogne speranza, voi ch'intrate or "Abandon all hope, you who enter here"

The counter manager for this job was a complete mess. She hired me and gave me my schedule the following day. I worked for a week or so, and everything was fine. One day, while I was out shopping, I got a phone call from the manager asking where I was, and why I wasn't at work. I looked at my schedule and the rest of the conversation basically went like this:

"I'm not on the schedule for today."

"Well I changed it."

"Ok, but you kind of need to tell me when you change the schedule, because I have other plans on my days off."

"Well you're supposed to know when you're working."

"I do know, but if you change the schedule and don't tell me, how can I know, especially when you change it on my day off. Am I supposed to call everyday and see if you changed the schedule?"

"Yes, you're supposed to be here now and you can't be this irresponsible anymore."

"Umm, Ok."

A week into retail, and I can see where this is going. I soon found out how stupid she was, and figured she wouldn't be around long enough for me to worry. Before managing the counter, she was an account executive for a major fashion designer with no cosmetic counter experience. This was a big, new line in the store and they hired a manager with no counter experience. Apparently, after 9/11 she decided she wanted to work less hours and get her priorities in line. That meant take an "easier" job that did not require her to commute to the city, and be able to spend more time with the man with whom she was cheating on her husband. Her husband had no idea and I felt bad for him because he seemed like a really nice guy. I'm sure her four kids didn't know either. She must have really been spending all that extra time with her "family", because she wasn't at the counter half the time. She lasted about six months. I came to work one day and she was gone. We figured she was fired, because she was never there. The brown nosing assistant manager probably ratted her out, thinking he would get her job. He didn't and thank God!

Our next manager was transferred from another store and was the assistant manager from a bigger counter. She was a thirty-year-old woman, who still lived at home with her parents and was dating the same guy for about nine years. Her family was ultra conservative, and she was not even allowed to go on vacation alone with her boyfriend. They always went with one set of parents and couldn't sleep in the same room. When she would go out with him, they had to lie about where they were going so they could get a hotel. Their parents thought they were still virgins and they led them to believe they were. We went from one type of cowardly manager to another. She was also the second of three managers in four years! That's a really bad sign and customers feel it and know something is wrong.

In the meantime, the Manager of Retail Operations who had been with the company for about ten years quit. The person who replaced her was a true fag hag and hell on wheels. She had a horrible reputation as someone that is impossible to work for unless she liked you. The previous assistant MRO actually stepped down from her position and took a counter manager position in a department store. That's unheard of in cosmetics. That speaks volumes of how nasty this woman was to work for and with. Her new assistant was this gross, gay guy with a lisp and thick black, rimmed glasses with black, greasy, thick hair. He totally reminded me of the teacher with the Vaseline on his glasses in Grease 2. He was such a tool and he was there as her snoop doggie dog. He would always flirt with the gay boys that worked for the company, which would eventually be his downfall. He went too far with one boy, who turned around and accused him of sexual harassment. His termination was a big laughing stock and of course the good news traveled fast. When I heard the news, I wasn't even working at the counter anymore, but just as happy.

This new MRO actually hired my friend without even interviewing her. She just liked her makeup and probably thought she was hot. She also paid her more than everyone else and let her order products above and beyond all the other employees buying limit. Most everyone under that MRO's region either transferred out or quit the company. It was very sad, since a lot of those people were with the company for 5 to 10 years. That's like twenty years in cosmetic years. She's the type of person who goes to a company promising them she can turn the sales around, and double sales overnight. She did this by scaring everyone into selling, or getting everyone to quit and replacing them with fresh new blood. This doesn't work long term. You need experience, dedication and consistency to sell and be profitable. The turnover and her reputation spread so quickly throughout the region and cosmetic world, that in less than two years, she was canned after they realized she did nothing but bring morale down. Sales were never the same after that either. I actually have nightmares about her coming to be my boss at other jobs.

One of my trainers with this company recommended me for one of the trainer positions in New York. She told me that I should try out for the position of trainer, and that I would be great at this job. I immediately sent my resume to the corporate office for this position, since I was looking to become a trainer and get out of the everyday selling. I got a call from corporate to come in for an interview for the position of trainer in New York City. A week after the interview, my MRO came to see me at work. She proceeded to tell me that I had no business trying out for that job, because I was totally unqualified and I didn't have the talents or ability to perform that job well enough. If I was so unqualified, why did the corporate office ask me to interview? In the meantime, I was working part time at the counter and had one of the highest sales numbers. I was the liaison between the counter staff and product development. I developed the events, and had professional makeup experience like ESPN, Olive Garden and Ladies Home Journal. She was so mean, I actually cried. Trainer was a job I really wanted, and she just told me I'm basically an unqualified retard.

Not long after, I eventually did get a training position with another cosmetic company. I made more money and traveled from Toronto to Pittsburgh. At one of the trainings, I was talking to a trainer from another company. I asked her if she knew the MRO, who I knew was now working with her company. "Oh yes", the trainer said, "She is one of the trainers for this area as well." Not only did I become a trainer like she said I never would, but she was now basically demoted to the same position I was promoted to! Needless to say, I hope we never meet again.

Slow Death

The public can sometimes be difficult to deal with on a daily basis in a retail environment. Here are a few situations that service people have to deal with. If a salesperson doesn't know the answer to a question, the customer will put their hand up in the salespersons face to dismiss them. The people behind the counter are not lying about being out of stock of something or sold out. Customers would sneer and ask for the manager, just to check if the salesperson knew what they're talking about. In one mall, there were three of the same cosmetic counters. People would stalk all three, ask the same questions to everyone and compare answers. They would ask about a product then say, "Well the other girls at the two other counters said something different." So go to the person who gave you the answer you want! I mean honey, its makeup. If you mix and blend well enough, you can probably wear any color lipstick. But a funny thing happens. After a while you start to act like the customers towards everyone else. It's easy to get petty and argumentative. This is when it's time to go, and find another job, or you'll start to argue with clients and that's a recipe for disaster.

If cleanliness is next to Godliness, then there are a lot of heathens roaming the cosmetic department. There is very little research done on just how filthy cosmetic testers are, but lipsticks and lip glosses have been shown to have staphylococcus and E–coli. Think about all the women with herpes on their lips that use the lipstick and then someone else comes and uses the same lipstick. How about people that cough on their hands or don't wash their hands after going to the bathroom and then stick their fingers in the eye shadow, powders or jar creams. Pink eye is often spread by everyone using the same mascara wands. Even my mother used to get pink eye when I would sneak her mascara as a kid. Kids with bugger fingers always stick their hands into the cosmetic testers. I used to frequent a cosmetic store in Manhattan that had a lot of homeless people wandering into it and I frequently saw them using the makeup testers with their fingers or using the brushes available. Even if they use disposable wands, there is no guarantee that a customer didn't double dip. It's amazing how people just don't care or think about major germs. I'm definitely not a germ freak; these are just basic rules of cleanliness.

One day a customer came to the counter and asked if there was someone there to help her pick out some colors. I told her, I could definitely help her. She looked me over, studied my face and angrily said, "No, I don't want you. You have blonde hair, and I have brown hair. I want someone to do my makeup that has brown hair so they understand what colors to give me." I just looked at my coworker and gave her the nod to have fun with this whack job. I really felt like saying, "You stupid bitch, don't you see I have an inch of dark brown roots, and I'm actually a brunette?" I sometimes wonder how this attitude would work with other topics. Would you refuse a kidney transplant, unless the doctor operating on you had a kidney transplant? Would you not let a hairstylist cut your hair, unless they had the same hairstyle you wanted? Could you imagine a stylist with all their clients looking exactly like them?

Here is another annoying thing retail workers complain about. Some customers stop at the counter and say, "Bobbie Brown." Of course they're asking where the Bobbie Brown counter is located. Retail employees find this method of asking so disrespectful. Are we so loathsome, that you can't speak in complete sentences to our face? Some workers would just look back at them and say, "Clinique." The customer would look with shock and or confusion. Then the customer would make the huge effort of adding "where is" to "Bobbie Brown." Some people would just say, "Yes, what about Bobbi Brown?" This would force them to actually phrase a question. Can you see how one could go mad working in retail? It's easy to become passive aggressive after so many hours a day of this game.

The fact that there was more than one of the same counters in the same mall did not mean they would lower the sales goals. In fact, when you reached any goals, the reward was higher goals, and the expectation that you would meet and/or exceed them. Cosmetics, is a "no win" situation. The company has no promise to help promote and advertise, in order for you to reach those goals. I have worked for a few companies, who thought it was beneath them to advertise. Then they wondered why their business was less profitable. It's because other companies are advertised on every corner of New York City. It becomes a staple of the shoppers' collective unconscious. Competition is fierce. And that is the appropriate use of the word fierce! My one friend who worked at a department store in New York City said that every salesperson had a certain amount of space at the retail counter. They drew imaginary lines from the counter to the entrance of the cosmetic department. Any customers, who walked between those imaginary lines, became your client. Whoever made eye contact with the customer first, got that customer. It's extremely cut throat and thus the reason people hound and attack you in department stores. The goals are unreachable and these women think nothing of taking off their Gucci stilettos, which they can't afford anyway, and tripping a coworker for a sale.

I had one coworker, actually accuse another coworker of the same sex, of sexual harassment. She said that her coworker touched her butt on numerous occasions behind the counter. This seemed completely insane to all the other workers. We all worked so closely together, I don't see how this happened at all. When corporate was alerted, they did absolutely nothing and told them to try and work together. It was big drama, and both of them ended up quitting. Working with them after that, was no easy feat. I had another coworker who was such a brown−noser; he actually took notes on what all of us did at the counter on index cards, and gave them to the manager. This moral judgment was coming from a man who was cheating on his boyfriend that he was living with! One day he left the cards in the office, sticking out of his brush belt. I saw it, and I had to take it and read it. It gave the dates and times that some co−workers came in late and if they went over break. Again, this was coming from someone who would go shopping during work. Karma is amazing though, because the company totally used him as a tool, but never promoted him. He tried for every promotion the company had open, and he got turned down for every position. I never really understood that since he was such a "company man." I think they felt if he was such a tool, eventually he would turn on them as well. That's just what corporate people do.

Gay−Trance

The cosmetic department is where I learned that gay men are GOD in the beauty industry. Women listen to whatever they say and whatever they tell them to do! It's the most amazing phenomenon I have ever seen. It's like a hypnotic trance. I call it GAY−TRANCE. Pitty pat, pitty pat! Patty pit! Patty pit! Ok, let me let you in on a private joke. When I was a young girl, my mother and I were walking through the cosmetic department, and there was this flaming gay, guy, putting eye cream on a woman. He was tapping his fingers along the eye area saying, "pitty pat, pitty pat, patty pit, patty pit." That was how he taught women to apply eye cream. My mother and I stopped dead in our tracks and couldn't believe what we were hearing. It was so funny, and to this day we still laugh about it. Remember this was in the late 70's or early 80's. The overwhelming gayness was striking in the suburbs at that point.

Years later, when I was working for Adrien Arpel, I told this story to my boss and she got all excited and said he was the old makeup artist for Adrien Arpel. She said, "Yes, he was an over the top drama queen to work with, but he had the women lined up and they couldn't get enough of him." His numbers were so big they had no choice but to keep him. As time went on, corporate did not ask him to do their events anymore. He got no retirement party, and no thank you, for the millions of dollars he made that company. Just no more calls to work and do what he loved to do and did very well. Sometimes the beauty industry *ain't* so pretty.

Gay–trance can't be beat by any woman on the planet. Get over it now and deal with it. A gay man can walk up to a complete stranger on the street and say, "Honey, oh my *gawd*, you need to fix those eyebrows. Follow me right now." The woman will look up with doe eyes and say in the ever so bashful voice, "I do?" Then she'll then follow him blindly down an alley on the old 42nd street of the 1970's, if that means he'll give her the next best beauty secret. If a female salesperson even mentions to a customer that she can help her create a better-shaped brow, the customer will say in a Gestapo voice, "Oh, so are you telling me there is something wrong with me? Who are you?" Some women are so incredibly insecure, it's very sad. It pains my heart to know that some of the most amazing women can't take another woman looking at them and trying to help. These are the type of women that do whatever a gay man tells them. Let me state this for the record. Not every gay man knows how to apply makeup, choose colors and do eyebrows! It's just like saying only black people know how to do makeup on black skin; same stupidity. Yes, gay men are better than your average straight guy in makeup and beauty, but that doesn't mean they are the end all.

Gay–trance is incredible to see in action. We would just stare and watch the male makeup artists to see if what they did was any different. There was no difference, but the women would buy all the products they recommended. Sometimes we used the gay men to close our sales. If we wanted to quickly close a sale, we would bring a gay guy over ask his opinion. Of course they always say the woman looks "fabulous" and she would whip out the credit card and say, "Ok I'll take two." That easy! If a gay man can't close you, you aren't in the mood to buy. Go eat some ice cream and come back later. I highly recommend going to the mall and watching these men work. Now that you know the truth, you'll see a whole book on the psychology of gay–trance waiting to be written. Get to writing, you fierce bitches!

Taking Inventory

Inventory time is always stressful and just plain crappy. Basically, we had to count every piece of makeup at the counter and in the stockroom. This is a day everyone dreads and a day you never call out sick unless you want your coworkers to hate you. No one wants to go, but you go for your coworkers. The night before one inventory day, I was deathly ill. I was throwing up all night and the only sleep I got was a few minutes leaning up against the toilet. The next morning, I got up from the floor, took a shower and went to work. I told people from the other counters that I was sick, and to come and get me from the back stockroom, if any customers really needed me. About 15 minutes later, they told me a girl needed help picking out a lipstick. I stumbled out to help her, and as I was talking, I said, "I'm sorry, I'm really sick, I'll be right back to help you." Before I could turn away, I fainted. Yup, right there in the middle of the cosmetic department, I fainted. Thank God some girls from the other counter noticed I was really sick, and happened to run over to catch me as I was falling face first onto the tile floor. My coworkers told me that right after I fainted, the customer immediately turned to the girl who caught me, and asked if she could help her pick out a lipstick. My coworker was shocked and said, "Can't you see she just fainted? Come back later." I wouldn't be surprised if she went to management and complained about bad customer service. As soon as I woke up from fainting, I jumped up, puked bright yellow liquid and walked to the back room to rest! Of course the cute security boy was standing over me. How mortifying.

Afterward, a really strange thing happened. That night, no one from work called. The next day, no one from work called. Then the third day someone finally called, and it was the brown–noser who used to rat on everyone! Never in a million years would I have expected him to call. We weren't really friends, especially since I was pretty close with other people at the counter. Neither the counter nor cosmetic manager called to see how I was feeling. Now explain to me how someone faints and pukes yellow liquid in the middle of their job and the manager never calls to see how they are feeling. There were only four or five of us at the counter. I was really shocked and then thought about why this happened. Was it because she hated me so much, and she didn't really care? Could she be so socially inept, she didn't call to see if I was ok or ended up at the hospital? Either way, I gained a lot of respect for a man with whom I was not even friendly. I also lost a lot of respect for the counter manager who never called to see if I was ok. You can see why it was a revolving door of workers in this store.

Eww Baby Bus

Let me explain the "eww baby bus." Every night the eww baby bus would come to our cosmetic counter. We sold a lip gloss named Oh, Baby. This particular gloss, when combined with a lip liner called Chestnut, looked, shall we say, "fierce" on darker skins. It was always a winner and the go–to product when someone with darker skin came to the counter. Obviously, many black women came to the counter to get this combination or at least the gloss since it looked great alone. Every counter across the country representing this line, experienced this phenomenon, and it was really funny to see in action. At the end of the night, the department stores were open later than the mall, so the last ½ hour of the night could be your busiest time. On any given night, you could have a group of black women approaching the counter and we would look at each other and know exactly what they wanted. Someone would say, "Here cooooomes the eww baby bus," and sure enough, they would come up to the counter and say, "You got eww baby and chess–nut?" Classic! At the end of the day, it didn't take much to entertain us, but an eww baby bus.

Mommy Dearest

It's amazing how many mothers think the cosmetic department is a childcare bubble. Let me describe a typical scenario. A woman approaches the counter, with kids who have had it with hours of shopping, and now close to being out of control. This is what the woman customer is thinking as she goes through the cosmetic department with her kids. "Who cares if they're bored, tired and unhappy, I want a lipstick." So the kids run all over the cosmetic department, with no one watching them. The mother starts trying on lipsticks, five minutes go by, and the kids are yelling and running around. She then tells the kids to stop running around. The kids don't listen, and keep running around crazy. Another five minutes go by, and she might say it again, but with no authority and the kids know it. She is completely obsessed with herself, and takes for granted that no one will steal her kids, even though everyday in America, children are stolen right out from under their parents nose. No one in the cosmetic department cares about your kids. They're busy with their own customers because they have goals to meet bitch.

Eventually, the kids are quiet because they are getting into something potentially dangerous. The mother is now happy, because the kids are quiet and once again, she can concentrate on herself. This was the most frustrating thing to observe. Sometimes, I would say something like, "I think I saw your child walking out the door into the mall with their father." Of course I knew the father wasn't there, but who could resist snapping this unqualified parent out of her cosmetic haze. Did all the fragrance in the air freeze their brain? Sometimes they would yell for their kids and get no response. This was always good, because then I would say, "Gee, I hope he wasn't kidnapped while you were trying on lipsticks. That happens all the time in the mall you know." Of course the mother would get somewhat frantic and slowly start to remember that she had children. Women, get a babysitter and don't torture your children with shopping.

Custom Blended – Just For You!

My friend worked for a counter where they custom blended foundation. Her coworker had a customer who treated her like crap, and she finally got tired of being abused. To get back at her, she started spitting in the nasty customers foundation as she blended it. One day, that same customer came to the counter to pick up her foundation. As she approached, my friend noticed that same customer was her neighbor! She never told the customer her foundation was being spit in. She did say she was a high maintenance bitch, but we both agreed that spitting in someone's foundation was over the top.

The Bitch Still Owes Me Money!

Fresh off the eww baby bus, I gathered my makeup kit and brushed myself off. I interviewed with the owner of another cosmetic line, in her New York office and I was thoroughly impressed with her savvy and spunky personality. She looked at me with shrewd squinting eyes as she determined whether I could make her money or not. In the cosmetic world, I knew just what that meant. Fakey fake, air kiss. Very L.A. Here we go again. In order to work for her, you have to become like rain man with her "selling talk." You must use her words with co–workers, as well as customers to describe products. It was all very scientology–like, but I was close to broke and what the hell. Maybe I had finally learned how to act "as if," and pretend to be a good corporate soldier.

My interview process consisted of working for free for three days selling her products, on which I had not been trained. On my first day, I went to one department store. Now I didn't particularly care for this store, but I was willing to do it for a day. To my surprise, the brown–noser from my last counter job and another makeup artist I used to work with were working in this store. When I told them what I was doing, they both looked at me as if I told them I actually DID become a Scientologist! They both agreed that I would never be able to last, given the horrible reputation of this line in the cosmetic industry. This owner had a well–known reputation, for being one of the worst people to work for in the industry. I tried my hardest, because I know I'm good at what I do, and I really wanted to get her respect. The second day, I went to another department store and sold my butt off.

The third day I went to a Soho store. While I was there, I noticed a rather muscular, large, hot male, makeup artist coming towards me to introduce himself. I told him what I was doing and he grabbed both my shoulders and said, "Honey, don't do it. Don't work for that bitch. She'll never pay you. Don't you know her reputation? The bitch still owes me money." I laughed, and said I knew of her reputation, but I needed a job. She is relentless about the numbers, and nothing else matters. She was known to call her sales people at night to ask them why they didn't sell more or reach their goals. What do you say to a phone call like that? It was raining, and no one came out in the tornado to buy a makeup kit?

After the three days of working for free, I sent her a card reporting how much I sold at the end of each day. My numbers were great, and I had complete faith I would get the job. I did get the job, and I even negotiated five more thousand dollars a year. She did pay well, but that's so you'll hopefully stay and deal with the constant harassment. Every penny had a trade off. My job as a regional makeup artist was to go to three different counters in one mall. I was responsible for selling make–overs and events. It was basically an easy job, except reaching the huge goals they give you. They give you big goals, so you can never reach them. This way, they can fire you whenever they want if they don't like you for any reason. My goals for each day were higher than the counter goal itself. That of course makes no sense whatsoever! That is how the industry works though. Every company is basically the same. My goal was approximately $1000–1400 a day in makeup sales aside from the counter's goal. The daily counter goal during the week was usually about $500. Hmmm, now I'm really bad in math, but something doesn't seem right here!

My first day at one of the counters was interesting. I still wasn't trained on the products, but I was sent out to work until the next week when training would take place with the national trainer. When I met the counter manager, she asked me to take a walk. We walked to Sephora, where she went in and talked to the store manager about an interview she had there. It was shocking that she took the new regional artist to another store, so she could check the status of her interview. Hey, that would be bold even for me! She easily could have been reported back to corporate so I could gain major brownie points. I understand that retail can really suck, so I basically kept to myself. Business can be slow, and it's hard to pull clients. Attacking browsing customers is not my style. I don't want to be like the fragrance nazi's. That's the spa part of me. Once you come to me, I give my all in selling, but I really don't care for stopping people in the middle of the aisle and asking them if they want to try a new eye shadow. In order to be successful in that type of environment, you really need to be a good puller. My first week went fine. It was short lived.

During my second week, the new hires were trained on the products by the national trainer. There were about ten of us. We sat around a table and the trainer went through all of the skin care products and how amazing they were because the owner's husband was a dermatologist. If her husband was actively involved with the formulation of the products, I would never use him as my dermatologist! As far as I was concerned, the products were a complete scam. They're overpriced, and totally ineffective. As I was reading the ingredients on the products, I could see this was the case, but I kept my mouth shut. UNTIL, the trainer got to the Vitamin C cream. She went on and on about how great the Vitamin C cream was, and how great Vitamin C was for the skin. I asked a very simple question that anyone with half a brain would ask. How much Vitamin C is in the Vitamin C cream? Her face had a look of a deer in the headlights and she said, "Well, we really don't focus on one ingredient specifically. It's really a great cream, and all the ingredients work together." "Ok", I said, "then why call it a Vitamin C cream, if you don't focus on one ingredient. The percent of Vitamin C does matter, because there has to be a certain amount of Vitamin C in order for the cream to work and be effective. Do you happen to know the pH of the product as well? If the pH is too high then the Vitamin C is ineffective. It will neutralize the acid and not work." She told me we would talk about it later.

At this point, she had it with me, and her look told me all I needed to know. This was part of the whole scientology type talk that I was busting open. When speaking with clients or coworkers, you have to say the exact phrase for each product and repeat it like a drone. With every client that comes to the counter, you have to say that her husband is a dermatologist. Most customers will never ask these burning questions about percentages and pH. That is why horrible, ineffective cosmetics, creams and skin care sell. It's all marketing and companies know this sad fact. That's why she really pushed the fact that her husband was a dermatologist. People really bought it and believed it, especially if you say a New York dermatologist. It's like the clincher if the customer shows any doubt. It's the equivalent of gay–trance.

After letting these pesky little facts go, we moved onto the next issue. The trainer had a hard time saying one of the main ingredients in one of the products. She kept trying to say hylauronic acid and she couldn't pronounce it correctly, and didn't know exactly how and why it was important in skin care. I graciously stepped in and pronounced it correctly! I even explained what it was and how it worked. This training was so elementary I couldn't stand it. It's like a research scientist not knowing how to pronounce centrifugal force. It was complete bullshit, and I could never, in all ethical soundness, sell this skincare. I figured my days were numbered and so my old habit of just speaking my mind came back. That was always a bad thing if I planed on keeping a job!

Later that day, we moved onto working with the colors. I figured this had to be better, since she was known for her colors and makeup, not skincare. I was wrong. I was coming off a very creative line with great makeup. To start this part of the training, we went to the counter and started doing makeup applications on each other. The owner has very specific ways to apply makeup and very specific brushes to use for each step. As an artist, we take great umbrage with someone who tries to tell us exactly how to apply the makeup and give exact steps. All artists use different methods, and all are great and worthy. The colors had no pigment and we were told that the makeup should never really be seen. Well that wouldn't be a problem, since you couldn't see the colors when you put them on anyway. "What if someone comes to the counter and wants smoky eyes", I foolishly asked. "You can do it, just very light," the trainer told me. My eyes must have rolled with such a stupid answer. Smokey usually means dark, not light. That's like giving someone baby pink lip–gloss when they ask for red matte lipstick.

It got worse though. We were told to use a specific foundation brush to apply the foundation. I tried applying the foundation, but the brush kept separating and left brush lines on the face. In frustration, I stated to my partner that the brush was horrible. Of course the national trainer was standing right behind me, and that sealed my fate. Three quarters of the way through the day, we were all taken aside and given our schedules. The guy before me told me he was confused, because he was given a territory he wasn't expecting to get. He got my territory! I knew my upcoming meeting meant I was going to get the ax. As I went upstairs to get my "upcoming schedule", I was given my walking papers. They said that in the past, if the artist didn't like the products, it usually didn't work out. I plead my case and said I would just need some time to adjust to a new line. They insisted that I would not fit in with their company and ideas. They let me keep the handy make–up holder, and I use it all the time. I keep my heavily pigmented eye shadows in it! Thanks bitch, kiss kiss. PS – I did get paid in full for the time I spent working for the company! The guy who got my territory hated it and quit two weeks later.

Down N' Dirty

When you work with the public, umm, shall we say, after a while, nothing will surprise you! There is probably no story that would make me say, "Oh, my god, I can't believe that happened!" Public workers become desensitized, like kids who grow up watching violent movies and *gangsta* rap. So when you're in a store, and you wonder why the $10 an hour person really doesn't care about your traumatizing decision over a reddish pink lipstick or a reddish orange lipstick, get over it! Just pick a friggen lipstick lady and try watching your kids who are tearing up the whole department! Selling can be like dating. It's all about trying to get the richest guy or hottest girl. It's a game, and women absolutely love this game of being told to buy something, so they'll feel better. Shopping highs can last longer than some relationships. We absolutely have clients we really like. Yes it happens, and a genuine connection is made. I have had some amazing clients who have helped me along the way, taught me about my strengths and weakness and made my job worth going to. Let me restate for the record, that I have had many more good experiences in this industry than bad. This book shows the not so pretty side of the beauty industry.

Working in a spa lends itself to dealing with peoples bodies! This can be a double–edged sword. Of course we all love the hotties that come in to see us and get groomed! Since I'm not a lawyer, shrink or teacher, hell yeah, I have gotten involved with a few clients. They're the only men I happen to come in contact with, that aren't gay! Thank god for metrosexuals. Men tend to be better tippers and less demanding then women. They're just happy to be taken care of, and pampered. I have a few specialties I perform in the spa. One happens to be Brazilian or full bikini waxing. I consider it my "pubic" service to men and mankind! When men hear I do this service, their eyes get all wide and the drool starts dripping. They of course have visions of lesbian love and hot wax! *Trust me; waxing women has reinforced my heterosexuality.*

So many women come in paranoid and profusely apologizing for their unclean, smelly or hairy body. Those women are usually totally normal, clean, and healthy beautiful women. Society has convinced them that they are in a perpetual state of needing to be fixed. If your legs are hairy when you come in to get waxed, it's ok. They're supposed to be hairy in order to wax them. Lip and chin waxes are done in almost every spa around the world, because 99% of women have hair on their upper lip and chin. *You are normal.* It's the women who are really gross and dirty, that never notice their nastiness that I'm writing about. It's amazing that the dirtiest women tend to be the wealthiest. I have no clue why this is, but the only thing I can think of, is the lack of respect for others who have to deal with them. One place I worked in New York was in an area where the women played tennis all morning and afternoon. So how does this effect one working in a spa you wonder? Well, they play tennis for a few hours, sweating to death in the sun with tight spandex shorts suffocating and fermenting the sweat in their cooch. Then they come to get waxed, before they go home to shower. Um, excuse me? This is like eating a few cloves of garlic, drinking beer, smoking a cigar, and then going to the dentist. Get the idea? It got so bad, we actually had to put baby wipes on the waxing table, and tell the women they had to use them and wipe, *before* we waxed! One place I worked in New Jersey, had women that liked to ride horses. Riding horses properly is one hell of a workout, but now add the smell of horse into the mix. Neigh–thank you!!!

Yes Ma'am

I took my job search to the internet and found a spa the south looking for a lead esthetician. The job said it paid $1700 a week! Now in New Jersey, that's a lot of friggen money, but in this part of the south, that's mega bucks. It sounded way too good to be true. So of course I applied! The owner and I spoke a few times over the phone, and she eventually came to New York to interview me.

At lunch, she proceeded to give me the low down on everyone working in the spa and whom she wanted me to replace. Oddly enough,

I have been known as "the cleaner." If you're trying to squeeze someone out of your business or boost sales, hire Lora. Throughout lunch, she kept drinking alcohol and I kept drinking my ice tea! The more she drank, the more she started to open up about her boyfriend who came with her on the trip to New York, and how he was not really the guy for her. It was a sign of the drama to come. I was fully aware of the insanity, but when an opportunity to make money comes, you take it. She kept telling me how busy she was, and how busy I was going to be. After my years of knowing how shady spa and salon owners could be, I had a feeling she could be way over estimating how much money I could make there. If most girls in New York aren't making $1700 a week, then how can it be done in the south? Maybe since there wasn't much competition, she was capitalizing on the market. I decided to give it a chance on a one month trial. If I liked her and she liked me, I would then fully move down there. I drove down there, with big dreams and big promises. We agreed that I would stay in her guestroom until I found an apartment. I lived with her and her daughter for the time being.

With muzzle in hand, I started working at the spa. It was a nice place, with mostly her clientele and vacationing people. My co–workers were not very friendly. I noticed this immediately and thought that was not typical of spa people. I knew I was on their shit list because I was taking clients from the other esthetician she wanted to squeeze out. That's usually what spa owners do. They won't fire you, but they will stop booking you, and put all the clients under someone else's name. So you sit there all day, making no money and wonder what you're doing there. One day I asked the owner why they were so unfriendly to me. She said they all told her they didn't want to work with someone from the north and they didn't like Yankees. "Wow", I said, "I thought the enemies were the terrorists, not a girl from Jersey." She said, "I'm telling you this because I know you'll understand how some southerners are, since you have dealt with this before. The people from this area in particular, are much closed to outsiders." I thought that comment was very funny, since none of the staff was originally from that area. They all grew up in a different state or forty–five minutes away!

This whole "hating of northerners" thing is so stupid to me. It just adds to the whole idea that southerners think that northerners think they are stupid. Well to be honest, people like that, do nothing to help their cause and only perpetuate that assumption. I would like to enlighten the southern part of the country. No one in the north ever talks about the south. We never talk about the Civil War past fourth grade. The south has not gotten over it and is still living in the past. One thing I found to be really ironic, was that one of the black co-workers didn't like me because I was from the north. Now explain to me how a black man is going to be anti-northerner. Excuse me, but if it wasn't for the north, you would be getting me ice tea and calling me *massa*! Has the south really been all that great to you?

The owner was a great esthetician, but definitely not someone who should be managing people. This presented a host of problems. Her goal was to hand her clients over to someone else, so she could concentrate on building the business. That's a great idea, but very difficult to accomplish in reality. Most of her clients have been going to her for many years and only wanted her. Some clients will change and some will not. I started to see a pattern there that worried me. She was not that busy! If she was not that busy and she was the owner, how was I going to be busy? I quickly began to wonder how I was going to make $1700 a week. I was glad I was at least smart enough to demand a $500 a week salary to start. Needless to say, I never really made over $700 a week out of the month and half I was down there. I have no idea how she ever came to the figure of $1700 a week in straight commission. When I first asked her for a salary, she told me I was crazy, and that I would be begging to go on commission after a few days. I would make twice as much money on commission than salary. For once in my life, I took the safe and secure route and asked for salary. Once I was settled in at the salon, I went back in the appointment book and looked at how well the other esthetician was doing before I got there. I started asking around to coworkers and people in town about how the spa was doing and its reputation. I was shocked when I learned how many people had worked for this woman and quit. I also learned that no esthetician was making that kind of money. I tried to think positive and went to see some apartments. I kept thinking, I have been here a few weeks and she writes the paycheck every week. She knows I'm clearly not making anywhere near $1700 a week. Does she really think I will financially be able to move down here and that I would really want to move down to make less than half of what she promised.

It was easy to see why her establishment was a revolving door. In my opinion she had an issue with alcohol and liking it a little too much. She was also frantic because she was in debt with one business while trying to open a bigger business. She was one of those people I really wanted to like, but as I got closer and closer, I realized she was pretty toxic. When she did do something nice, I felt as if it was only to make up for something bad she did previously.

Not long after my arrival, the owner got very sick with some kind of stomach problem. I think it was an ulcer that was flaring up. To stop the pain, she drank a lot of rum and coke. I think that's what doctors recommend for ulcers, especially when you couple that with ulcer medication. Her boyfriend at the time did his best to comfort her and try to get her to not drink. There wasn't much I could do, since I was living with her for free and she was my boss. I was like the gay, little Asian houseboy that had nowhere to go but the streets, so he lets the fat old guy piddle him and then pass out. Since she was sick in bed, she asked me to drive to Florida to get her daughter from her ex–husband. Mind you, I never even saw a picture of the daughter or ex–husband. She gave me the keys to her Mercedes truck and I drove to Florida to get the daughter. That was so strange and I felt so bad for the daughter because I knew the insanity that was her mother. It was a bit of a mommy dearest situation to say the least.

One day a girl walked in to apply for a massage position. She was a great therapist with a lot of advanced skills. The only problem was that she looked like she walked out of a commune. Titties swinging low, only to be topped off by her mustache and armpit hair longer than Julia Roberts'. Could you imagine hairy armpits hovering over your face as you get a massage? In order to get hired, the owner made her promise to wear bras, wax her mustache and clean up her clothes. That was some kind of public service or charity work, because that girl was from the Midwest and didn't say "yes ma'am," but she hired her anyway. Obviously, she didn't last long.

Another day I had a client come in to get a brow and lip wax and lash tinting. She and her boyfriend were waiting for me in the reception area of the salon. They were sitting on a bench slobbering all over each other, and drunk. I recommended that we didn't take her since she was clearly intoxicated. The owner instructed me to take her in the room and give her the services she requested. I started to tint her lashes, and as I was waxing her, she passed out. I continued working at that point because I was so pissed off. It was money in my pocket, and my pockets were close to empty. As she came to, she started to lovingly rub my arm and moan sexually. As I pulled away, she got startled and said, "Oh, I thought you were my boyfriend." I finished her service and sent her on her way. I had to look around for cameras. This must be candid camera, right?

In the time that I was there, a few staff members had come and gone. So many nights, the owner was drunk, or brought a different guy home. Some nights, she was actually with her boyfriend. She was constantly accusing people of stealing from her or lying to her. She was always the victim. Yet at the same time, she presented the picture of a strong successful woman, who did it all on her own. She's a successful, single mother, who was proof that if you put your mind to it, you can do anything. Many of the salons clients were vacationers, so they didn't know that the staff was always turning over.

After a month and a half, I told the owner that I would be leaving because I didn't make the money I expected to make in Georgia. She told me that, it was my fault, and that, people didn't respond well to me because I didn't say, yes ma'am. "That is what people respond to down here and that is what people want", she said. I had visions of that scene from Howard Sterns, Private Parts movie, where Pig Vomit was teaching Howard how to say WNBC the correct way. Then I thought, well if you know that people in the south only want someone who says "yes ma'am," then why the fuck did you hire a Jersey girl with a heavy Jersey accent? Why did she fly all the way to New York and interview me, when there were plenty of southern girls she could have interviewed. I was always stunned by that comment. I was soon informed that almost everyone in that area had worked for her or knew her bad reputation. That is why she was posting on the internet. She ran out of victims in the state of Georgia.

After giving my resignation, she proceeded to tell everyone that I was leaving because I missed home and didn't like Georgia or the south. It was a total fallacy, but I knew to keep my mouth shut long enough to get the last paycheck. I liked Georgia well enough, and my only real goal in going there was to buy a nice property. I can be put almost anywhere making $1700 a week and be happy! She put another ad on the net, and she asked me to interview and train my replacement. I thought it was interesting she wanted me to do that. Whatever dude. If it means another paycheck, I'll gladly do it. I found a nice girl who was from Georgia, with a thick southern accent and said, "Yes ma'am." She lived a few hours away and was going to take the room I was staying in, until she found a place in that area. Sound familiar?

It was an interesting spa to work in, to say the least. We had a great older esthetician from the south who said, "Yes ma'am" as well. She was also an alcoholic. One day, my replacement was training with this woman. She sat in the room and watched the older woman give a facial to a client. When the girl came out of the room, she pulled me aside and said she thought something was severely wrong with the esthetician she was learning from. I asked her what was wrong, and she told me that the woman was waving her hands around in the air like she was conducting an orchestra as she reached for the products, before applying them to the clients face. She would spin in circles in the chair and wave her arms around! She was clearly drunk or drugged. I couldn't help but laugh at the insanity and think about Ronald Reagan's trickle down theory. Crazy started at the top in this place, and trickled straight down.

I told the owner what happened, and she said she knew that this woman was a recovering addict. She had all kinds of money and boyfriend problems. She had court dates and called out sick many times. During one lunch break, the whole staff was talking about different places to go dancing, and she just walked in with her flask and started singing, "everyone in da club getting tipsy." We all just bust out laughing hearing this fifty something year old woman singing a song like that with a drunk, southern accent. Another day she went to the bank where the spa did its banking. She told the teller that the owner told her to get money out for her. The bank was suspicious, and called the spa owner to ask about this situation, because it was just too bizarre. That was the end of that woman working there. I guess in the end, the "yes ma'ams" were not worth it!

The girl I trained to take my place after I left, kept in touch with me, and told me the horrors of working there. It was good to hear that

I didn't lose out on a great opportunity. The owner married the guy she brought to New York, after cheating on him and talking behind his back. She said that the owner had to marry him, because she needed the money. She was close to being bankrupt, and would have lost her home and business, unless he gave her the money. The girl also told me a story about how one day the owner went to a psychic, and the psychic told her this esthetician was going to steal all her clients. The owner got totally paranoid and went to the esthetician's new apartment while the esthetician was sick, and convinced her to take a bath to feel better. While she was in the bath, she went through all her drawers and files looking for client names and started accusing her of wanting to steal clients. This girl couldn't hurt a fly, and was completely horrified by this bizarre behavior. The girl quit soon after, and went back to the other side of Georgia where she came from.

There was a really hot guy who used to come in for massages. The owner gladly massaged him, and she got all giddy when he was on the book. The staff always wondered if something else besides massage was going on with those two. He was married and seemed like a good, simple southern gentleman. He just didn't seem like the type to cheat. I never gave it much thought, and I figured the owner knew better than to risk her license by getting freaky with clients in the actual spa room. She was seriously dating her boyfriend, so I figured she wouldn't mess things up considering how everyone there talked about everyone else's business.

A few months after I left, I got a call from the spa owner. She told me that that the wife of the hot guy she massaged, found out they were messing around and told everyone in town. The wife actually came to the salon and started yelling at her in front of the staff and clients. She thought it was funny, and had no remorse over what she did to the wife, or her salons reputation. She then told me that she wanted to try out for Donald Trumps show, The Apprentice, and that she wanted me to write her application since she liked my writing style. I told her I would think of something to write, and I never spoke to her again. It was a very strange call, and I began to wonder what I was doing in my life to attract such crazy people!

Movin' On Up

Upon my return to New York, I found a job immediately. I worked as an esthetician in a retail store with treatment rooms. The first week of work consisted of training and on the first day, I drove to New York, parked and went to class. When I came back to the parking garage, I realized I was nine dollars short in cash to pay for parking, so I went to the ATM to get more money. Apparently, you can't take money out of the ATM for less than twenty dollars and all I had was twenty dollars to my name at that point. Ok, I thought, I'll charge it, but the parking garage didn't take credit cards. I was shit out of luck. I knew a look of panic must have come over my face and then some elderly woman from Virginia gave me the nine dollars to get my car out of the parking garage. I felt like such a loser for having less than twenty dollars to my name. Accepting help has never been a strength of mine, but this was a great lesson for me. Sometimes I can't do everything myself. It's ok to ask for help and ok to accept help. And of course it's important to say, "Thank you."

I loved this job and loved the opportunity to work with what I thought would be business people, instead of spa people. I absolutely loved the products so it made selling quite easy. If you've been paying close attention to what I have written so far, you'll know there is always a catch. We received commission on the products we sold and we were supposed to get the commission check every two weeks to a month. They hadn't figured out the exact payment system when they hired us because this store was so new. With every month that went by, we would ask for the commission. Every month they would say, "Just be patient. We are working on it and trying to get the best formula." We figured they were just trying to get a history of sales numbers to see how little they could try and pay us. Seven months went by and I started to lose my cool. One day I was talking to a coworker who was still friends with the recently fired coordinator. This former coordinator found her job listed on Monster.com while she was still working at the job. I felt badly since this person did her job well and the new director was just going to replace this person with his friend. This new regional director fired almost everyone and replaced them with his team that goes everywhere with him. That old coordinator told my coworker that the corporate people had no intention of ever paying us. Well, that was all I needed to hear to set me off. I mean, we were doing our part in good faith, and expected the same in return.

The next morning, I went online at the front desk to find the phone number for the Department of Labor. I told my assistant manager to immediately call the corporate office to tell them I wanted my check by the end of the week. I told her I would call the Department of Labor and picket in front of the store saying this company doesn't pay its workers. New Yorkers absolutely love a good picket line. I was really angry since the check was for approximately $1,000.00 per esthetician. She knew I wasn't joking. She said the corporate office told her that our checks would be there in two days. My store manager at the time knew they wouldn't arrive, but didn't tell me she knew. She led us to believe our checks would be there. When two days came and there were no commission checks, the screaming commenced. I also knew the checks weren't coming because my coworker overheard the manager telling someone that the checks weren't coming. So I gave them till the end of that week to get the checks or all the estheticians would picket in front of the spa and call newspapers, the Department of Labor, and anyone else who could help us get our money. We would also bail on the already booked appointments until we got the check. At this point, they knew we had enough. With me leading the pack, they better pay up. The money was Fed–Ex'd to us the next by 10am. If I knew it was that easy, I would have threatened to picket a few months earlier. That was one of my better Norma Rae moments.

They also tried another cute trick. As estheticians we did facials and body treatments even though it was in retail store. After a few months of working there, the owners suddenly said they didn't want us to get tips. When we were hired, tips were never even mentioned. As an esthetician, if I'm doing treatments, I'm getting tipped. It became a huge issue, on top of the fact that we were still working without getting our commission checks. We had meetings and conference calls regarding this matter. The owners had the new director come in, and say that, "The treatments are not the focus, and since you already get a salary, you should not get tips." This reminded me of the Vitamin C cream discussion from my previous job. If the treatments aren't the focus, then why have expensive menus printed up describing the treatments, and why have all the beauty editors in New York City come in for free treatments. Why even bother hiring licensed estheticians? What the owners really said behind our back was, "If a customer is going to be spending money in our store, it is going to be on us, not the estheticians." Their attitude said it all in terms of respect. They actually wanted us to tell people that we didn't accept tips. "As if!" I would rather be fired then not take a tip. If I ever choose to not take a tip, it's on my terms and for my reasons. Again, we all threatened to quit and we won. My mother always called me Norma Rae and I guess she was right. I just can't take injustice. I'm far from perfect, but some things are just wrong.

There are a lot of crazy people in the world and many find their way to New York! I had one client who was a whirlwind. She had wild, crazy, long, thick hair. She carried a big designer bag that you knew she was using for shoplifting. She was always late, in a rush, smoking like a chimney and demanding she get whatever she wanted. Older, unattractive, wealthy men always accompanied her. She treated them like shit, but they loved it because they had a decent looking girl to make them look good. A note to all men; everyone knows the hot girl is with you for the money and it doesn't make you look cooler, just more ugly, older and pathetic. This client always stumbled in, hung over and would moan out loud during the treatments while I was massaging her. A few times during each treatment, she would try to pull the sheets down to expose her breasts, and I would take the sheet and cover her breasts back up. Every time she came in, she would steal a lip conditioner, anti–aging serum or shampoo from the room. I told the management and I recommended that we don't let her back. They said, absolutely not! She is allowed to come and get treatments. So every time she came in, I had to completely empty out all the drawers and products from the room. She would open all the cabinets and drawers and take whatever was left. If one thing was left, that's what she would steal.

I also had another client who was the mother of a very well known rapper. She was very well off through him, and a very nice lady. At the end of the body treatment, she actually asked if she could have the shower cap to take home! That was a first. It was some shower cap we got from the grocery store, but the only one I had left. I was kind of shocked, so I told her I already threw it in the garbage to make her think we didn't use the same shower cap on every client. We in fact did use the same shower cap for any client that wanted to use one. If she was a fanatic recycler, I could understand, but she just wanted to take it home. Maybe that's why she never tipped me.

Karma being what it is I knew it was only a matter of time before these corporate fucks had to pay up where it hurts. About a year or so after working at the store, the other full time esthetician and I quit. The trust was completely lost. There was no respect for us, and it was clear. Eventually the spa part of the business became very slow, and now they only have one person doing all the treatments and she isn't fully booked. I will say this: she gets her commission in a timely manner, and takes her tips home every night. She still thanks me when I see her!

Around 3am one morning, I got a phone call from a friend. He was calling to tell me that he was in the basement bathroom of a gay bar with the owner of my company! He asked, "Lora, did you know he is gay?" I had no idea, but suddenly it all made sense to me. The owner was a very good–looking man who dressed impeccably and was into skin care and perfume. How could I have not known? The clincher was that the owner was married to a woman and had children! They always portrayed this happy, blissful marriage, where they also worked together, very Bill and Hillary Clinton. When I finally did meet his wife, I was confused at the match to say the least. He was very good looking and fashion savvy while his wife was unattractive and frumpy. It now made total sense in my mind. I totally expected his wife to be a very trendy, fashionista like him. I guess opposites really do attract.

I started to think back about the owner and one conversation came to mind where he and the regional director were talking about a woman who gave building permits for one of their new stores. The owner called her a bitch and the director readily agreed. It sticks out in my memory because of the way he said it and the tone in which the director who was assumed to be a closet gay agreed with him. It was just a very strange vibe. I'm not easily offended and I'll be the first to curse someone out but it just had a whole other undertone to it. At the time, I thought he was anti–women, not anti–pussy.

In the beginning, they tried to hide the fact that he was gay. In the cosmetic world, nothing can really be hidden for very long. If you go to gay bars, fuck around with other men and are married, they can't wait to "out" you. Every gay man's dream is to out a well known, supposedly straight man. All gay men think other hot men could be, or are gay, if only given the chance! No one is going to stop buying your soaps if you're gay. Not long after his coming out, a memo was sent around the company saying that if anyone talked about the owners' personal business they would be fired. I still use, love and always highly recommend their products. I really loved that job and it's a shame they got greedy.

Caddy Shack

Now, for my Caddy Shack moment; yes folks, I have a doodie story. So there I was, working on the Upper East Side of Manhattan, when this very good–looking, John Kennedy Jr. looking guy came in to receive a body treatment. Let me set the stage for you. I walked the client into a dimly lit room, told him to get undressed and under the covers as soon as I left the room. I massaged his whole body using aromatic oil. This was a relaxing massage to put the client into a deep state of relaxation as opposed to a deep tissue massage. Next, I rubbed the client's full body down with a hydrating body scrub to exfoliate the dead skin. Once fully massaged and scrubbed, I wrapped him in heated blankets to help the oils penetrate. After twenty minutes, I returned to the room, unwrapped the client, and instructed him to take a shower in order to remove all the scrub. After showering, he could get dressed and come out to the front since the treatment would then be finished. At the end of the hour and a half treatment, he was very relaxed, bought some products and left the store.

When I went back to clean the room, I picked up a towel and there was a big, brown streak on the once pristine white towel. I just looked at it and thought, "Could it be? No! Oh my God!" So, of course I had to sniff it, thinking it must be melted chocolate he was eating in the room to finish off such a decadent treatment. Maybe it melted in his pocket and he wiped it on the towel. It could never be actual shit! But yes, it was shit! So there I was, standing alone, holding this shitty towel with a look of disbelief on my face. I was trying to visualize how this happened. What were the circumstances? Did he know he did this, and if so, why would he leave it there? Did he wipe his ass too hard after showering and come up with a big, doodie streak? But who has that much shit left over in their ass–crack? I'll never believe he had that much shit left over in his ass. He must have known there was that much shit on the towel, since he just left it there like a prize. Maybe that was my tip for a great treatment. Was that how he felt about the treatment? Was it shitty?

I promptly brought the towel out to my boss and said, "If there is ever a day you think I get paid too much, this is the reality of a day in the life of a spa worker. This is what we deal with, and this is how some people treat us." There were corporate office people in the store that day, so they were completely aghast and shocked. The corporate people only see pretty rooms, relaxing treatments and smelly candles. No one ever thinks there is another side to spa life. I have to admit, I wasn't too shocked. It was really only a matter of time before I got shit on, literally.

So if I got shit on, you know I have bloody cooch stories as well. Let's get back to the small percent of women who make my job very interesting. No, sorry, I don't want the privilege of waxing your bloody vagina. Is your period natural? Yes! Is it normal? Yes! Do I want to wax you while you have your period? Hell no! Just because you have a string hanging out of your hole, doesn't mean you're clean enough for your Brazilian. Women have leaked and left blood all over the sheets. It's really gross when women have bloody underwear when they come to get waxed. We even offer them disposable cotton underwear to use during a bikini wax, but they actually choose their blood stained ones. Let me tell ya girls; a big, puffy pad is no secret either. You know what, I wax them anyway. That's what happens when you work on commission. Wasn't there a movie called, For Blood or Money? Well, when you're on commission, you do both.

Crazy Bitch

"Hire the best. Pay them fairly. Communicate frequently. Provide challenges and rewards. Believe in them. Get out of their way and they'll knock your socks off." – *Mary Ann Allison*

I was brought in to work at a spa in New Jersey with the old manager Micky. It was a beautiful spa. The manager wanted me to come on board because her staff, in her opinion, was extremely rebellious, lazy and irresponsible. I was brought on as a full time esthetician when there already was one working there! Yes, I was brought in again, as "the cleaner." This is how managers and spa owners work. If they don't like you and want to get rid of you, they stop booking you, and book someone else.

Everyone in the spa knew I was friends with the manager, and that I was hired to squeeze out the other esthetician. I really felt bad about this since she was a nice girl and had been working there for a few years with an established clientele. Everyday the esthetician would come in, and I would have all the new clients as well as some of hers who were willing to see me. Sometimes the manager would tell clients the other girl was booked and they could see me instead. Of course the other esthetician knew what was going on, and it put me in a very uncomfortable position. It's survival of the fittest, and I'm a survivor. I wasn't making fast friends, but I tried, since they were really nice girls. I quickly saw how the manager was so wrong, and her staff was actually quite good. They just had it with her antics. Right before I started, there were so many complaints about the manager, her boss had to come down and interview all the staff one by one, and get their side of the story.

Eventually, one day it came to a head, and the esthetician stormed into the salon and rolled her skincare machine right out of the room. She was yelling and screaming at the manager as she walked in and out of the salon with her supplies. It reminded me of the opening scene in the movie Life as a House, where he smashed the model homes with a baseball bat! I felt bad to a degree, but at the same time when she left, I took her title, her health benefits and her clients! Within the next month or so, almost the whole staff that had been there for about three years quit. I knew it was going to be a crazy ride, but the advantages of me being there, outweighed the negatives. Plus, I met some amazing people who changed my life for the better. It was a time for me to grow and learn to give better customer service and come out of my shell a bit from the previous few years of social hibernation. I was in a major personal funk the past few years before this position, and now I was finally ready to let it all go, and start to fulfill my potential. I started to be social again and I really needed this visible position at that point in my life.

After the other esthetician quit, I got the title of Director of Esthetics. Since the manager was so needy and scattered, I was able to really implement my ideas and take over many projects to put another notch in my business belt. I was able to develop new treatments, events and specials. I was also able to help write the list of services and website. I spent many hours helping for free, just to get the experience and say, "I did that before." Little did I know I was being prepped for when I opened my own business.

In a twelve month time span, more than sixty staff workers came and went. This was a salon with a staff of approximately fifteen people so you can see what kind of insanity I'm talking about. The manager there had a bit of a love for the drink! Eventually, she lost her license and I ended up picking her up everyday at her house and drove her home every night, for six very long months. Do you know the bitch had the nerve to be late half the time when I picked her up! Finally, I had to actually say, "If I get up an hour early to come here and pick you up, you better have your ass out on the stoop waiting for me as I drive up." It took me a half an hour to get to her house and at least a half hour to go to work and then a half hour to take her back, and then another half hour to get to my house each day. Why did I do something so stupid? Loyalty, friendship, and dedication, that's why. As crazy as she was, I thought she was my friend, and I thought wrong. She never told her family about her DUI and I never told them either. She told the staff of the salon that she let me drive her everyday, so I didn't have to pay for parking at the spa. This was obviously not true. She was the queen of manipulation.

Driving her was horrible. She was completely paranoid and thought every truck that was driving close, or a mile away was going to hit us any second. Many times I wanted to go out after work but couldn't, because I had to drive her home. She could have easily rented a room near work and walked. It was pure torture for me. The first day she got her drivers license back, she gave a coworker a ride home. On the way home, she told this person that I wasn't selling enough products because all I thought about was men. She said that I was distracted and not focused at work. Maybe I was exhausted from the extra two hours tacked on to my already long workday in order to drive her drunken ass home. She was also comparing my sales numbers to another esthetician with over twenty years of experience. I had approximately 7 and 1/2 years experience at this point. She actually had the nerve to call me a few days after she got her license back, to tell me that I was not selling enough products and I should focus on work more than men. I felt like telling her she should focus more on work than drinking. Or maybe she should focus more on retaining staff than having them leave after a month or two of working with her.

Since I wanted to learn more about the business side of spas, I spent a lot of unpaid time trying to learn as much information as possible. I worked on the website, menu, events, networking, ordering, inventory, advanced classes, etc. Somehow I wasn't focused? Working with my boss was so difficult, because she had the attention span of a gnat. I would spend so much time finalizing details of a project, and then she would completely change her mind. This made it close to impossible to finish anything, and eventually, I just gave up and said, "You tell me what to do and I'll do it. "I'm not going to come up with any more ideas." This was taken as a negative attitude, but it was really that I had nothing left to give her. I was drained and she knew I hit the wall with her. At this point, she started saying that I was no longer interested in being the Director of Esthetics and that she can make someone else the Director if I wanted to back down. I told her to, "Go ahead and make someone else the director! There isn't anyone! I'm the only person willing to work for you full time and I'm about at the end of my patience with you." She knew I was right and that she needed me more than I needed her.

I relinquished my endless hours of working with the manager to the part time esthetician, with twenty years experience. They had the same outcome. The other esthetician was a bit nicer in the beginning when they disagreed. Not long after, they had it out. The frustrated esthetician ended up going out for lunch and never coming back! This was a common occurrence here. One manicurist girl left for lunch and never came back or called. We were actually kind of worried about her because she had an abusive boyfriend. We looked in her manicuring drawer and everything was gone. That meant she left, and knew she was never coming back. There was another hairstylist who started working at this salon for three years, and suddenly cut all his days down to one day, after this manager took over. He had a very loyal client base and many would go to the other salon he worked in just to see him. Then he started calling out a lot. Eventually, he just never came back, and about three clients from his huge clientele stayed at the salon. One hairstylist went on vacation and never came back. Another girl who worked there for years and had a full client book called out sick a few days in a row and never came back! She actually moved to another state. She never gave notice, and never told the manager that she was unhappy there. That was becoming the norm there. Just pick up and leave. One massage therapist came in drunk or high one day, walked out and never returned. The manager tried to get her to come back because everyone was quitting and a drunken massage therapist was better than no massage therapist in her mind.

It got so bad, the manager hired people without even doing a practical on the interview. Her reason for hiring one girl without doing a practical interview was, "She kissed my ass and it's about time someone around here kisses my ass." This backfired every single time. She once hired an esthetician because her ethnic background matched that of many of our clients. Another got hired just because she was pretty and cheap to hire. She was seventeen, married and she paid her $10 an hour with no commission! I heard her interviewing her and telling her she would get health benefits (when I knew there were benefits for only four employees already working) and that she could be the director of esthetics one day (that was my title). When people started there, they all thought I was mean. I really wasn't, but the joke was, if you stay more than a month, *then* I'd learn your name. Until then, you're just "that new girl." She would hire completely unqualified estheticians and then ask me to train them. After a while I told her "No mas." I'll teach someone the treatments and protocols, but I'm not teaching someone how to be an esthetician. One girl even put water all over my face with a peel on it. That's something you would never do, because water deactivates the peel! Someone right out of school should know at least that much.

So many crazy things happened at this spa, that it's painful to actually rethink it and rehash old drama. The manager had quite the reputation for drinking and hooking up with guys once she was drunk. It was actually starting to ruin my reputation, since we had to spend so much time together. I actually heard from a coworker, that a bartender from a nearby bar, said that the manager and I had a threesome with someone else who worked in the area. Great, how do you deny something like that? No one will believe it wasn't true when your friend already has a bad reputation.

Here's a cute trick she would do. Have a staff of employees that are only booked half the time. Then she would hire a new therapist and promise them the world. This world included health benefits, free gym membership, and a full book. The new person would come in and then get no bookings or very few, because the person already working there was promised the same thing! Then the new person would get mad at not being booked solid like they were promised. Then the manager would shift certain clients around, so the new person would be getting some clients. When clients called, the front desk person was told to put them with the new therapist, at the same time the old therapist was already booked. This made it look like the new customer wanted that specific time and had to be booked with the new therapist. This would create great dissention and mistrust between the staff as well as the staff and manager. The manager did this with the thought that if the staff was divided, they couldn't gang up on her. She thought it would motivate the staff to work twice as hard. Obviously, with the turnover rate she had, this wasn't working. This is actually a pretty common practice in spas and salons. The owners or managers get so scared to lose one eyebrow wax, they hire more staff, so every minute of the day is over covered just in case. It sounds logical, but if the staff is willing to work on straight commission, you should fully support them and not take money out of their pocket. It's a bad business practice on many different levels.

One time we were having a staff photo and she purposefully neglected to tell a certain staff member that we were having photos that day, because she didn't want her in the photograph. The girl had a big afro and the manager didn't like it. This girl was a great therapist and her clients loved her. We were all dressed in black, and this girl was dressed in her beige massage clothes ready to work. Eventually, she figured out exactly what happened. This was yet another turning point in my opinion of my manager as a manager, a friend, and human being. Is this someone I want in my life? Hell no. This was disgusting, and I felt awful for the therapist who was so nice and willing to stay and work, even after that!

After our friendship was over, Micky told one of my clients over the phone, that if she booked her facial with the new esthetician, she would give her 75% off the service. The client said, "No thanks, I prefer Lora even at full price." The client thought it was really fishy and told her hairstylist about it. Then the client told me about the manager's offer. I thought my head would explode, but I said nothing so as not to put the client in the middle. I just told her, "Well you know how nuts the manager is." She laughed and readily agreed. I was tempted to tell the client that her $150 microdermabrasion treatment was actually a drug store microdermabrasion cream for $5, not the one we were advertising, but I kept my mouth shut. The manager loved advertising one thing and replacing it with something from the drug store. This was the first of three times the manager made this offer to the client. The client never accepted.

Our spa had the worst reputation for staff turnover. Eventually, I had to confront the manager with this little tidbit of information and she denied it. Then she said, "I can tell the client to go and see whomever I want." "Of course you can", I said, "But when the client tells you to stop harassing her to go with a new esthetician, you should stop asking her. Besides you are supposed to be my friend. You even made my parents pay full price when they came here to get massages, yet you give a client 75% off just so you can try and screw me? Do you really have to wonder why, over the past year, 60 staff members have come and gone?" "Are you actually keeping track", she said. "The whole town is. You are the joke of this town and everyone knows that everyone leaves here because of you and only you."

One time I filled out a request for a day off. She approved it and then wrote at the top of the sheet. "Lora, where is your coverage – this is hurting our business and the policy is to find coverage." At this point in the spa, there was only one other esthetician working there, and she was part time and worked at another spa the other days. So whom was I supposed to get coverage from? I was literally, the only esthetician. There were no coverage options. I told her, "If I am the only esthetician working here, I can't ask anyone to cover me. Does that mean I can never take days off?" "No, of course not, just get coverage because I can't have no one working in a department." "Ok, but do you realize I am the only person in that department? Whom should I get coverage from?"

She huffed and puffed and said, "Well, for the future, get coverage." Ok psycho! This is how many of our conversations would go. She only heard what she wanted to hear. If everyone didn't keep quitting, maybe I would be able to request someone to cover me.

There was another time I was supposed to go do a charity event for a few hours during the day. It was in the morning and I would be back in the early afternoon before we got busy. My manager had a two-month notice, and was ok with me doing this event since it was with a company we had a very good working relationship with. A week before the charity event, she called the person running the event, and told them I was unable to leave work and that I never got coverage since I was so irresponsible. I was horrified, since I knew they would never find someone to replace me so fast and I was only really missing three hours of work. Funny thing is, anytime my manager wanted to do promotional stuff before, during or after work hours, I was always there. I did events where I was unpaid in addition to doing events during work hours, so I couldn't book any clients. I called the person running the event, and told her I was coming anyway, and to act as if I never called to tell her this. I also told her to be prepared for my manager to call her and ask her how I did that day at the event. I told the charity event planner that my manager was crazy and would try to trick her into admitting that I was there. I knew my manager would know I was there when I called out from work. Like a textbook, my manager did the exact thing I knew she would. The charity event planner called me laughing and thanking me for the heads up. She also thanked me for being a person of my word.

I'm sure we had to be one of the only salons to get kicked out of a national spa program. We participated in this program and had great success with it. One day we got a call from the people at this program and they said our spa didn't pay them. I heard the manager say, "The check is in the mail." I could tell she was lying, because she froze at the front desk. When I asked her about it, she said she could take care of it and it was the accountant's fault, so mind my own business. When this manager took over, she wrote many bad checks. In less than a year time span, she had over $800 in bad check fees! Eventually, the corporate people started to cut her budget, but she never stopped spending. Everyday, the people from the national spa program would call and she would not take their calls. Eventually, they called and said we could never participate in their program again. She had a habit of not paying people, and changing the agreements she made when they didn't suit her needs anymore.

Since the spa was not doing well financially, the corporate office told her she had to do treatments. On Sundays, she would work in my room when I wasn't there and leave a mess of cotton, dripped wax, and spilt bottles. Then on Tuesday, she would come in and yell at me for a dirty room. In the meantime, I wasn't there the past two days! She would put the tweezers in the barbicide jar upside down and then complain that I was wasting $20 tweezers by denting the tips. I got smart, and kept my own tweezers and made everyone else use the dented ones, until they got the idea that I didn't even use those tweezers. Towards the end, clients were always moved from my column and into someone else's. I would go to the front desk, and move them back into my column before she noticed. I would also run up to the front desk and take the client into my room. These were clients that were already mine, and would walk right up to me expecting to be seen by me. How could they see me not busy and then go to someone else? It would never happen. You don't let just anyone touch your body. She would put clients with another therapist and not tell the client. She would hope they would see someone new in frustration and then get used to seeing that person.

On many occasions, she would ask staff members to do services they were not licensed to perform in order to make a few bucks, and not lose a sale. This is a big no–no, because if someone finds out or something goes wrong during the treatment, the whole spa could be shut down and fined. One day it finally caught up to her. Someone called the state board they came in, and fined the spa, her, and a few unlicensed staff members. Consequently, one of her most profitable hairstylists had to leave the salon and never come back. Another one of my friends needed a job, so I told her to work at this salon on Sundays. She was an esthetician and didn't do nails. The owner wanted the day off to go out with her boyfriend, so she asked the esthetician to do pedicures. The esthetician agreed, even though she is not licensed to do pedicures. She had no idea how to do one, so the manager put yellow sticky notes with numbers over all the products, so the esthetician would know the steps for the pedicure. I wonder if the esthetician took the stickies off before the client arrived. That esthetician lasted a week, called out sick on a full book and never came back to work. Since I could do so many services, she always tried to get me to do deep tissue massages or manicures and pedicures. Most everyone by now knew the managers reputation, so I couldn't convince anyone to work there anymore. I think I was just looking for a friend to work there to validate the insanity.

She also tried to screw me on commissions for sales of products. Many of my sales were either given to someone else by mistake, or to no one at all. She gave me such a problem with getting this money. I made her go back almost a year in sales and figure out what was mine or not. She actually told me that it was my fault, that I didn't train the front desk how to do the commissions right. I'm an esthetician, not the spa manager, the front desk manager or the assistant manager. Why would I train the front desk? This was money I made for the spa, and money I rightly deserved. I never asked for anything I didn't earn. I am a good enough seller that I don't need to steal sales. These corrections boosted my sales numbers, and proved that I can sell, meet goals and think about men at the same time.

Since this was a bit of a Peyton Place, clients as well as coworkers were also involved in her demonic web of deceit. One day she asked me if I thought that one of the hairstylists was selling cocaine to one of our clients. I told her I had no idea, and I didn't even know if they talked outside the salon. The conversation ended there. A few months later, the hairstylist told me that the manager said that I accused him of selling drugs to that client! I was shocked. At the same time, the manager hired this same hairstylist's friend to work the front desk on the weekends. She told me that she didn't want to hire the friend because they could easily make a deal to steal money, clients, products or services from the spa. She had to hire him because everyone else had quit, and she wanted to go away that weekend with her new boyfriend. The poor guy was never trained and thrown into the lion's den with no preparation. When the hairstylist told me that she said I accused him of selling drugs to clients, I had to tell him what she said about hiring his friend and what was really going on. That hairstylist became fast friends with the manager, so I knew he would immediately go back and tell her what I said. We all knew that the relationship between the hairstylist and manager would be short lived since they were both shady and manipulative. The staff would even tell him false stories and see how long it would take for him to tell her and for her to come out of her office and ask someone if something was true or not.

In every day spa, candles are a big part of the ambiance. Low lighting is essential for a relaxing environment. If a salon has candles, they obviously need lighters. Everyday was a fight to get lighters or matches. Every day we complained that there were no lighters, again. A normal manager would go to COSTCO, and buy a huge box of lighters or matches. Some form of fire! This manager told us it was our fault there were no lighters, and if we needed to light the candles, we should bring lighters ourselves. She said we should use our own money and she would reimburse us, because she shouldn't have to get everything. How could we expect someone who is writing bad checks to reimburse us? No staff members would bring in lighters, so we stopped lighting the candles. One day the corporate people came to check out the salon and there were no lit candles. She got right in her car, went to COSTCO and bought a box of lighters. End of problem. I know it all sounds silly and petty, but these are just basic things to run a spa. If you buy candles, you buy lighters.

She then got caught having sex in the spa with a guy who used to work in the area. She used him for years for free dinners, free parking and whatever else she could get him to do. He was the typical guy who loved being abused, but eventually, he did get to bang her. She left used condoms in the room over the weekend, and it wasn't hard to figure out who was using that room. About a year and a half after I left, the salon was sold to a new owner. He was very hands on, and shocked at the condition of the salon. He kept her for a few months to get all her information, help in the transition, then fired her. I feel sorry for the next salon she tries to manage.

Lego My Client

"Pretend that every single person you meet has a sign around his or her neck that says, 'Make me feel important.' Not only will you succeed in sales, you will succeed in life." – *Mary Kay Ash*

Stealing clients is a big deal in our business. You get hired in a salon, do really well, and build up a clientele. Then the manager's crazy side comes out, or you decide to open your own place. Whose clients are they? Well, it depends who you ask. Some places make you sign a no compete clause. This means that you wont work in a certain mile radius should you leave that salon, and of course you won't take any of the clients when you leave. I don't believe in this at all, and I would never sign one. I wouldn't even agree to not taking the clients names and numbers or contact them if I leave. Owners believe that anyone who comes into the salon is theirs. I understand their point of view, but I, as the therapist, am the one who keeps the clients coming back. I am the one they come to see to make the owner more money! It's like stealing someone's boyfriend. It's impossible to do. A man will leave if he wants to, if he feels there is something better out there. The same goes for clients. They will only go with the esthetician or therapist if they want to, and believe following that person is more beneficial to them, than staying at the salon. They might follow the therapist, and decide the new place is too far, or doesn't have the same amenities, and return to the first place. This is just the natural law of the salon and spa industry and the way it goes. In a business that has no health benefits, no sick days, and no 401k, our clients are everything. It's do or die with no guarantees.

Many times, I do believe that owners and managers get so greedy that they almost force the therapist out the door. Most owners see short term, not long term. Owners think that giving the esthetician a bigger percentage of the profit, takes money out of their pocket. In truth, the therapist is still making the owner more money then if they weren't there. Once that esthetician leaves, there is no income, and who's to say that the new esthetician will be any good or as good. Owners should give more commission, or find some way to compensate the person doing all the work. Estheticians and massage therapists really work their body hard, and are a limited resource. It is sometimes hard to take the owners side on this issue since I have usually been on the other side. I do agree with the owners that finding good, qualified, reliable workers can be very difficult. You would think after finding someone good, they would be grateful. Relationships are relationships I guess!

In New York the competition is fierce. There is a new spa opening up everyday by disgruntled estheticians. Sometimes they open up in the same office building as the spa they just came from. More often than not, they open up across the street in order to keep their clientele. This causes a lot of drama for everyone involved. The original spa owner then calls the clients and tries to give them cheaper priced services in order to keep them. Next, the owner will call the product line they are using and tell them, if they sell to the new spa, they'll dump the line. The skin care lines don't usually comply with the original spa because history shows, where the esthetician goes, the sales go. Even if there is some agreement with the line that they won't sell to a salon in a certain radius, they'll find a way to break it and sell to the estheticians' new place. Only if the salon has big sales, regardless of the esthetician, will the product line not sell to the new salon. I once had a former employer tell a product line they couldn't hire me for any position within that company, if they wanted to keep them as a client. It's all very Wall Street sounding, but money is money, no matter the industry.

Winter Wax

Here's another thing I don't understand. In the summer, all spas get inundated with bikini waxing appointments. So I'm sure you can see where this is going! What the fuck are these women doing during the winter? They don't wax in the winter? For years this baffled me, so eventually I started to ask my clients why they only wax their bikini in the summer. They said it's for their bathing suit and they just let it go in the winter. Ewww! Ok, so now I'm wondering if they ever thought of being clean in the winter for sexual or personal purposes. Do they not have sex in the winter? Maybe this is the real reason men love spring break and try to bang as many women as possible in the summer. It's the only time they can get waxed, clean pussy. Makes sense to me!

Waxing Big Women

Waxing an obese woman can be a really difficult process. Here is the problem. In order to do a good, painless wax, you have to keep the skin firm and tight. It's nearly impossible to hold the flabs of skin away from the bikini area, keep them tight, apply the wax, and grab the cloth strip and rip, all at the same time. The next problem is that larger women can't reach over their stomach fat to their thighs, to help you hold the skin, and they sure as hell aren't flexible enough to lift their leg up. Even if they could lift their leg up, it doesn't help much because they can't lift it that far since their stomach fat is blocking the leg from moving. Are you getting the mental picture? This is one of the hardest services to perform in terms of waxing. Of course I always get the obese women who want a Brazilian. I wonder if they're getting it because some guy is going to be going down there. Maybe she only wants a Brazilian to be cleaner and in vogue. If that's the case, then drop 100 lbs. I will always try to defer this type of waxing to someone else. It is very hard to do without bruising the skin, or end up sweating like a pig while trying to hold back flabs of fat.

Man Cooch and the Whole Ball Of Wax

No men, you can't escape from pube grooming either. Please return the favor, and buzz or shave down there. Wax if you wish, but we don't want a tangled mess down there either. My poor grandmother never had oral sex. One day, I just had to ask her. Grandparents are full of great information that will be lost with their generation. Maybe since no one was grooming down there, sixty years ago, they were better off not having oral! Younger men are into taking care of business down there. The rest are usually a big mess, like the women over forty! Unless you coat your pubes with mint for flossing while I'm down there, just buzz it down.

Waxing men can be a little painful. For them I mean. It gives me great pleasure to legally give men pain and get paid for it. Most of the area doesn't hurt to wax, but when it comes to the balls; it seems to be quite painful. I recommend shaving or trimming down the balls and wax the rest. I think most women just want it to be buzzed down, so it's not all over the place. Now, we're all for the ass crack waxing. You'll be amazed at the level of cleanliness you get from doing this. It cuts down on smell for men the same way it does for women. You don't need anymore junk in your trunk, especially if it smells.

Lora Condon

Politically Not So Correct

"I'm not running for office. I don't have to be politically correct. I don't have to be a nice person. Like I watch some of these weak–kneed politicians, it's disgusting. I don't have to be that way." –
Donald Trump

After dealing with so many different types of people, it is easy and amazing to see patterns in cultures and vocations. I'm sure I can get into loads of trouble with this section, but what the fuck! I have never been one to step away from controversy! If Jesse Jackson can call New York "Heimetown" and still be interviewed on CNN like he isn't insane, then I can give my true-life experiences. Here are a few observations from the past ten years experience in the industry. These are generalities, so get over it if you fit into one of these categories. These are just my opinions, and we all know what they're worth.

Female Lawyers

These women totally missed the boat on feminine hygiene and all things girly. I highly recommend that the majority of female lawyers get a stylist to tell them what to do. Listen closely, follow directions and don't argue with someone for once in your life. Trust me, just about anything you do, is an improvement. Put that money to use and invest in yourself, especially if you are an ultra–liberal granola lawyer. Pick up a copy of Vogue and learn that appearance really *is* everything. Then make Playboy your new bible, since you don't believe in God anyway and memorize it. Female lawyers don't need to wear red lipstick to look powerful. Just look at Hillary Clinton! She looks pissed and cranky, not powerful. Maybe it's just her crappy, crusty underwear bunching up, but red just doesn't work in the workplace. Lawyers are also just an annoying bunch to sell things to. They obviously know nothing about make–up and skincare, but feel the need to borderline harass you about how things work. Don't argue with me about why you need a gentle facial cleanser, instead of soap! Plead no contest, and acquiesce to the professional's recommendations. I rest my case!

Male Lawyers

Yes, the rumors and jokes are true! They're arrogant bulldogs, but better groomed than their female counterparts. They tend to go from zero to sixty when not served in a timely manner. They yell very quickly and are mistaken into thinking it will get them served faster and better. "I can make that back wax very painful if I want asshole! Speaking of asshole, you need that waxed as well today? I have it on special this month. It's bootyliscious baby!"

Asians

You can't sell them shit, unless it was made by an Asian company! They know somewhere around the world, they can get it cheaper. Many Asians keep their eyes open the whole time they get a massage or facial. This is one of the most disturbing things. They never relax. Whatever the reason, it's strange to be massaging someone while they stare at you the whole time. Even when I would be massaging their face, they would have their eyes open, as I would go around their eyes. All estheticians joke about this, and know how to handle it. Eye pads baby!

Another tip for Asians, your skin is not pure white. Sorry, get over it and buy a foundation that doesn't make you look like a geisha. Asians are obsessed with having pure white skin and always want to buy the foundation that is two to three shades lighter than their skin color. I'll sell it to you because I need the sale, but just try buying the shade that's right for you. They're usually crappy tippers as well. I think the whole super smart thing is just a myth because they never seem to understand the steps in doing skin care and makeup. I think that is why Clinique developed the three–step process. Asians ask you to repeat the cleansing process over and over. Maybe they just like to make fun of at the way we talk behind our backs!

Blacks

When white people are working behind the makeup counter, many times black people come up to the counter and say, "Can you do black skin?" Could you imagine going to a makeup counter with a black person behind it and saying, "Can you do white skin?" See how dumb that sounds! When a black person does like and trust you, they will be a client for life. They'll shank anyone who gets in their way of seeing you! White women are not loyal like that. They go around constantly trying different people, and always believe they can find the next best great person. Sluts!

Men

In the cosmetic department of a mall, men are so intimidated and scared. You can sell them a $200 foundation brush for their wife, and they will buy it just to get out of there! Men should really calm down because, the last gay thing you can do is surround yourself with single, beautiful women who want your money. Oh wait, that's the New York bar scene! But really, because we know men are scared, they get great service in the cosmetics department. They are almost always extremely respectful, courteous and grateful for our help in choosing the perfect gift for the woman in their life. We know she will just return it anyway, so don't sweat it. Men appreciate that we'll call them when we have a gift set or some great product, we think their woman will want.

In spas, men are the best clients in many ways. Here's a tip for men. You don't need to shave before a facial. It actually makes your skin more sensitive to the facial, but in a bad way. Leave the exfoliation to us. Men are just happy to be taken care of, with no strings attached. Most are very grateful, accommodating and good tippers. Men are like black people, in that once they like you, they will never feel the need to try another therapist. If you made them happy, why bother looking anywhere else! Too bad men don't feel like this in romantic relationships! Men as clients are almost always a good deal all the way around. They come to get the service with no emotional blackmail, like you get from some women. Some women really come in to get emotionally fulfilled from a facial or massage, whereas men come in to fix a problem and reduce stress. If the temperature in the room is a little cool for their liking, they don't complain to the owner and consider the whole treatment a loss. Plus I can date them!

Doctors

They truly believe that they should always be served first and taken in front of everyone else, "because I'm a doctor." I can't tell you how often I have heard that come out of their mouth. Being a doctor doesn't mean you can do whatever you want, and get away with it. If you need to cut the line, and it's so important that you get that lipstick, then get a personal assistant to run your errands. You have the money, as you continuously remind us! Don't leave the office or hospital if you only have twenty minutes to buy all your Christmas gifts on December 23! Back of the line bitch and I'll be happy to help you, after I have finished serving the ten people already waiting on line! Even Clinton, the most powerful man in the world, made time for a blowjob, so you can wait online to shop. I'm sure you didn't leave someone on the operating table to go shop! Wait on line like everyone else.

Teachers

Pick a subject and they have an opinion and something to bitch about. I think they're just trained to complain, even though they make pretty decent money, and get the summers off, and can't be fired no matter how bad they suck. Really now, every job has its good and bad, but they seem to focus on the bad. They travel, eat and shop in packs. If you get one teacher, you get them all. It's really an amazing thing. They have strong ties like cops and firemen. If you ever serve a teacher, you can be sure the other woman with her, is a co–worker. They aren't big spenders and are extremely picky. They're very stressed out people. Teachers are still pretty conservative in terms of fashion and beauty choices. They usually get the cheap and simple colors or services; very low maintenance. They also quiz you with tons of questions that lead to no–where like Asians and Indians. They're usually not great tippers either.

Indians

Dots not feathers! This has to be one of the most difficult clients. You will almost never make them happy, and you will always charge too much in their opinion. They will ask you a million questions just to annoy you. They have no intention of buying because they mostly only use homemade Indian stuff or Clinique. For some reason Clinique (which they pronounce clinic) is the cosmetic Promised Land for Asians and Indians. Good luck getting a tip from some of these tightwads! Most of them are only doctors, computer programmers or engineers which also makes them a very unhappy bunch that has no clue what would really make them happy in life. We have a saying in New Jersey. *Fuhgeddaboudit!* If you're an Indian man or woman, get a pedicure now. These people have feet that look like they walked right out of a Planet of the Apes Episode, from the 1970's. Don't look at your feet and wonder if you need one. The answer is yes! And tip that pedicurist 25%, for exfoliating those crusty metatarsals.

Spa Do's and Don'ts

Do's

1. Do relax. I can't tell you how many times I have been massaging people's hands and they are gripping my hand so hard.
2. Do tip 15–20% if you liked your service.
3. Do rebook and take care of yourself, more than once a year.
4. Do tell the therapist if the hand pressure is too strong or not strong enough. If you don't tell us, we just do whatever our normal pressure is.
5. Do make sure you book a deep tissue massage if you want a more intense massage with stronger pressure.
6. Do try different services, especially if you are comfortable with a certain therapist.
7. Do call if you are running late. They may or may not be able to accommodate you upon arrival.
8. Do tell your friends about the spa and therapist. We live off referrals and greatly appreciate them.
9. Do ask questions.

Don'ts

1. Don't be late
2. Don't expect sex, or hand jobs or blowjobs. We have a job already! There are plenty of places for freakiness in the

back of newspapers. Don't come, or cum to us with these expectations.

3. Don't take a long shower during a body treatment. That shower time, cuts into your treatment time.
4. Don't keep looking at the clock. Spa time is a give or take 5–10 minutes. How do you think we book on the hour and still clean the room, sell you, and talk to you on your way out?
5. Don't fault the therapist for things they can't control like the parking, receptionist, weather, temperature of the room, wrong booking, or hard to get appointments.
6. Don't wait till the last minute to redeem a gift certificate. Don't beg for it all year and then not use it.

Don't refuse to do or use what the therapist tells you, and then keep asking why your skin or hair hasn't changed for the better. We're beauticians, not magicians. Also, don't expect us to be able to change everything in one visit a year.

Beauty Bullshit

"Beauty always promises, but never gives anything." – Simone Wells

I would like to bust out some of the most common beauty myths. Basically, some very smart salespeople came up with a bunch of lies to get you to buy their products. Don't blame them. I'm sure their boss was breathing down their throat threatening to fire them unless they reached their goals. Every single person in the beauty industry has lied to make a sale. They have to in order to survive and sometimes the customer really wants to hear those lies. It goes back to the fact that most people, especially women, buy for emotional reasons. Some lies are so pervasive; the truth can sound like a lie. So bring on the bullshit.

You don't always need to use all the products from the same line in order to see results. Ingredients are ingredients. The skin doesn't know the difference between different labels. It knows things that work and things that don't. Only on rare occasions does the synergistic myth ring true and it's usually with professional products like peels or perms. Many skin care lines will tell you that you need to use their specific three–step system in order to have perfect skin. They market their products in this manner because they know the average person will only use three products on a daily basis to get desired results. Most customers complain about aging, breaking out and dry/oily skin, but don't want to really do the work needed to prevent or clear up these problems. The average person with no skin problems might only need three products and they are a cleanser, exfoliator and sun block. They can be from three different cosmetic lines. The products will never interact negatively. If you are doing a more intense treatment like a chemical peel or lash extensions, it may be important to follow all the instructions provided by the company to ensure consistent results. When I am applying Xtreme eyelash extensions, I only use the Xtreme products. I do this so if something goes wrong, it is every easy to eliminate the factors that made the eyelashes fall off. For example, if the client uses the Xtreme makeup remover, I know that there is no oil in that remover that might dissolve the glue. Another makeup remover might have 10% oil which will easily remove the lashes. I also only use Xtreme's glue because I know it has the best adhesion ability. Using cheaper or different glue will not give me the best or consistent result.

The active ingredients touted by the company should be listed in the first five or six ingredients. Ingredients are listed from first to last by the amount in the product. Please turn the box over and read what ingredients are actually in the product. The first five or six ingredients are the most active and important. The rest are not that effective. A vitamin e cream only works if the Vitamin E is one of the two or three ingredients. Obviously, the star ingredient should be listed first if that is where the company is claiming the results are coming from.

Sun block is not what makes you break out. It is the mineral oil or other pore clogging ingredients they put in the sun block. Find a sun block without mineral oil, petroleum, or lanolin or isopropyl palmitate like Skin Ceuticals or Dermalogica. Opt for a natural sun block like titanium dioxide or zinc for more sensitive skin. There is no such thing as waterproof or water resistant in terms of sun block. You must reapply sun block every one to two hours if you are outside in order to be protected. Unless you can see the moon, you must be wearing sun block year–round.

Most of the more expensive creams are some type of mineral oil, which is basically petroleum jelly. If petroleum were really that moisturizing and healing, we would all have the skin of a baby. One famous cream in particular that touts itself as a miracle cream is mostly petroleum jelly, irritating essential oil (putting eucalyptus oil around the eyes is insane. Think of putting Vicks around your eyes). Lanolin is fatty, yellowish oil from the wool of sheep and extremely irritating. To add insult to injury, the loads of preservatives might destroy any of the so–called miracles going on with the cream. If some of these creams did what they claimed, no one would have wrinkles, cellulite, dark under eye circles, hair loss, blackheads, stretch marks or shine. Yes, the opposite sex would run into your arms as the wind blew your cologne in their direction.

Just because someone is behind the counter, doesn't mean they have all the answers. If they're wearing a white jacket they probably know even less. They are trained sales people with goals to meet. Just because a Doctor recommends something, doesn't mean they have the right answer for your skin or concerns. Most dermatologists get fewer hours in cosmetically taking care of the skin than an esthetician. If the Doctor gives you a sample of a product you can get in the drug store or supermarket, it's because they need to empty space in the closet. Sometimes, they just give you samples to shut you up and send you on your way. Doctors might also get kickbacks from the company for promoting their products and writing prescriptions. This is not always the case and there are many good doctors out there, but at the same time, you almost have to be your own doctor and do your own research.

Just because a makeup artist's husband, brother, father, sister, mother or friend is a dermatologist doesn't mean their skin–care products are better than any other. It is mostly a marketing ploy to charge more for their products. Successful sales are based on successful marketing. Most people really want to believe whatever they are told by ads and salespeople. Sales and marketing people know this and will do whatever it takes to capitalize on people's desires. When I worked for cosmetic line that was owned by a woman whose husband is a dermatologist, we were told that with every sale we must continuously inform the client that her husband is a famous New York dermatologist and he helped her develop her skin care line. This line was filled with pore clogging petrolatum, greasy castor oil and an ineffective Vitamin C formula.

"All Natural" isn't always all natural, good or more effective. Poison ivy is all–natural! It's not a cure all, and once again, you have to read the label to see if it's really all natural or not. Don't be fooled by the pretty advertising pictures and tales of the poor people in the rainforest you're helping by buying their products. It's not too hard to walk into a store and turn the product around and check out all the non–natural ingredients. Alcohol is now used as an all–natural preservative. Yes, it is organic but we all know what happens when you put alcohol on the skin.

You don't have to have separate face, eye and neck creams. If you like the texture, use it anywhere. Traditionally, an eye cream has a heavier consistency than a face cream because it is more concentrated to go in a smaller area. If your eyes are very sensitive, you may choose a less active eye cream. Use a daytime moisturizer that is sun block. A moisturizer or foundation with sun block is usually not enough to protect the skin. True mineral foundation is the only exception. Now with so many mineral foundation knock–offs, it is imperative to read the ingredients and make sure it is only pure minerals and no talc or fillers.

Use your gut instinct when shopping for new products. If the claims sound outrageous, they probably are. Ask your friends what products they use and what has worked for them. Do some research on the internet about ingredients and try to find unbiased advice on skin, makeup and other health items. Do what feels right. If your skin feels really tight, dry or itchy after washing then you know that particular cleanser was too strong for your skin type. No eye cream is going to get rid of your dark circles. If they did, would anyone have dark under eye circles? Yes, you were lied to by the salesperson and yes even I lied to clients telling them the cream would work. I've got to make my sales goal.

Please stop with the free gift or gift with purchase gimmick. Just how many coral lipsticks can you use? Are you that desperate for shit you don't need? Please stop giving the free gift as a Christmas or birthday present unless you actually give the product you used to get the free gift. That is just so tacky and everyone knows what you did. You're not fooling anyone. Once my ex–boyfriends mother gave me the free gift from her Oscar de la Renta fragrance purchase. It was her favorite fragrance and the last thing I wanted to do was live some Oedipal fantasy while wearing my boyfriend's mother's perfume.

You know those beautiful mascara ads where they claim their mascara will give you long luscious, twelve–inch long lashes; yes, they're bullshit. If you look closely, those ads on T.V. as well as magazines are all fake strip lashes glued to the models eyelids. There is no mascara on the planet that gives you perfectly even and symmetrical lashes. This is obviously false advertising and I have no idea how the government lets these companies totally lie and deceive the consumer. I'm always shocked when I can see the ends of the lash strip curling up off the models eyelid. They're so brazen; they don't even bother to Photoshop the fake strip lash out of the picture.

Do you really think brunette Sarah Jessica Parker got her incredible blonde hair out of a $10 box? Try that and let me know how that works for you. That's all I'm saying.

The overwhelming majority of products that magazines recommend are from companies that BUY advertising space in that magazine. The next time you read a magazine and see they are recommending a beauty product, flip through and see if that company has taken out advertisements. If you don't see that exact product, you'll see another product from the same company and you might not even know they're a part of a larger company. The companies develop close relationships with the editors and then give them free products so the editors will say how much they love the product. The editor is a writer, not an esthetician or doctor. This leads me to my next point; no good doctor is going to recommend a drug store brand product to get rid of hyperpigmentation over a prescription brand. There is no way you can compare the two and drug stores are not even allowed to sell anything that would go that deep into the skin, so it's just a big scam.

When you look at the covers of magazines and they say to use these exact products to get the same exact look, they're usually lying. The makeup artist comes in and uses the products in their kit. If you've tried to reproduce the look from the cover of a magazine, you'll know exactly what I'm talking about. Since consumers have caught on, they now say, "this look was inspired by these products" instead of stating they actually used these products. The magazines promote their advertisers products so the cosmetic companies will keep advertising with that magazine. It's all very simple and that's why it's almost impossible for new companies to break through to the big time unless they're bought out by a larger company with connections or have a celebrity help promote them. If a small company has a celebrity endorsement, then a magazine will promote that brand. Celebrities sell. I'm sure a lot of magazines will try to rip me apart for this, and deny that it's true but I've seen this all the time working for cosmetic companies. Give them enough free services and products and they'll promote you. A magazine once approached me to advertise in their magazine. I asked them about the benefits of me advertising with them and they told me that they only do editorials on their advertisers. They also told me they only recommend products, services and anything else from their advertisers. It was a nice magazine but not worth the price. Advertising is extremely expensive and tends to show little return unless you're doing millions of dollars. I understand the magazines point of view. It's all very mafia, as in one hand washes the other. They should give special consideration to advertisers, but to consumers, those companies with the most money are not always the best.

Let me just say this again for the record. There is no such thing as safe sun. There is no such thing as safe rays. UV rays are UV rays and just because you aren't burning, that doesn't mean you aren't getting sun damage. The studies that tanning companies use to say tanning beds are safe, are done by the tanning companies.

I once did the makeup for an ad for a huge cosmetic company. The ad was for their new anti–aging cream. The model they used was a regular woman who gushed over how great her skin felt and looked since using the cream. That woman also happened to be the mother of the executive for that company. Do you really think that woman is going to say she doesn't love that cream and watch her daughter lose her job? So her testimony goes in the ad saying how much her face has changed since using the cream. In the consumer's opinion, testimonies can carry more weight than unbiased clinical studies. Plus they're a lot cheaper. Do you ever wonder who is paying for these studies to be done? Of course the study is done in the lab of the cosmetic company and they pay until they get a result they like.

Steaming the skin during a facial is just irritating and unnecessary. The concept is that moist heat will soften the skin and make extractions easier. This is true, but steaming actually has the reverse reaction. Too much steam dehydrates and irritates the skin leaving someone red and swollen at the end of the facial. Warm towels do the job just fine. If you have rosacea and the esthetician steams your face, run fast because that esthetician has no idea about skincare.

Microdermabrasion is a treatment in the salon where corundum or aluminum oxide crystals are blasted onto the skin and then immediately sucked up. The smooth result you get is because of the pressure and high–grade particles being used. Do not for one minute think that buying a home microdermabrasion kit is going to give you any kind of result other than a basic scrub. To compare it with microdermabrasion is blasphemous and they should not be able to make any comparisons whatsoever. If you buy these kits, just consider yourself one of the fools born every minute. Sucka.

As a beauty consumer advocate, I feel it is my duty to constantly inform the public as well as protect them and their hard earned money. It's disgusting what many companies, magazines and salespeople say in order to deceive you into spending money and buying their product. It is my mission in life to educate myself and others and force companies to higher more ethical standards. That was really the point of this book.

Most Common Complaints about Skin and How to Correct Them

Read The Ingredients And Get Knowledge – You must read the ingredients in your products. The first five ingredients are the most important. Anything after that is in such a minute amount; they probably don't affect the products performance that much. If they say it's a Vitamin E cream, and the Vitamin E is the eighth ingredient, that means there is very little Vitamin E in the product. The internet is a great way to look up ingredients and get an idea of how they work. Not everything you read on the internet is reputable, so I would definitely ask and confirm with your experienced esthetician. In all products, watch for mineral oil, isopropyl palmitate, lanolin, paraffin, petrolatum, petroleum, sd alcohol, denatured alcohol, talc, fragrance and isopropyl mystriate. These are also known pore cloggers or skin irritants.

Sun Damage – The only way to prevent sun damage is to wear sun block. Constantly! Some people say sun block makes them break out. This is not true. The other junk they put in some sun blocks is what makes you break out, not the actual sun block ingredient. If you're very sensitive, find a sun block made of titanium dioxide and zinc oxide. These are mineral sun blocks and tend to be less irritating. SPF only refers to UVB rays so even if you feel you are not burning; you are still wrinkling or getting skin cancer. Here are some rules for sun block:

1. You need sun block everyday that you leave your home rain or shine.
2. You need to reapply sun block every hour or two if you are sitting in the sun.
3. Nothing is waterproof. Always reapply after swimming or heavy sweating.
4. Find a sun block that blocks UVA and UVB rays. UVA rays cause skin cancer and wrinkles. UVB rays cause burning.
5. The SPF doesn't mean very much, and gives you no more protection from UVA rays if the number is higher. You still need to reapply every hour if outside, even if it's a SPF 60 to prevent UVA damage.

There Is No Such Thing As Safe Tanning In The Sun Or In A Tanning Booth. It Does Not Exist.

According to the 2010 www.melanoma.org site, every eight minutes someone in America is diagnosed with melanoma. One American every hour dies from melanoma. I wonder what people would do if this was AIDS. There are no big parades, colored ribbons at award ceremonies, or famous activists for skin cancer. All you young girls under 30, your chance of getting skin cancer is increasing faster than any other age group. What's Snookie going look like in twenty years? Love you Snook!

Dark Eye Circles

There are a few reasons people get dark under–eye circles. Some circles, you can change or make less noticeable. Some you just have to minimize through makeup and accept. Circles can be due to bad circulation, genetics, diet, medications, stress, smoking or using mineral oil based makeup removers and cleansers. I know a girl who had one colonic and her dark circles completely disappeared. If it is genetics, then you have to use a color corrector first, then a concealer. By using a color corrector, you neutralize the dark circle and then need to use less concealer. The most important thing is to keep the eye area hydrated. There are no oil glands around the eye area, and that is why it tends to wrinkle first; thus the need for extra concentrated hydration. A pure 10–15% Vitamin C serum is good to put under an eye cream as well. If your eye circles are blue based, use an orange color corrector. If your eye circles are more purple based, use a yellow color corrector. In terms of color theory, you are canceling out or neutralizing the color of your dark circle first, so you don't need to pack on so much concealer. This theory also works well for neutralizing the color red that shows up in pimples and broken capillaries. You would use green to cancel the red.

Flaky Skin

Flaky skin is due to dehydration. You can have a face full of acne, be extremely oily, and still be flaking. Water and oil have nothing to do with each other. It could be internal dehydration, which is due to not drinking enough water. Drinking too much coffee, alcohol and smoking severely dehydrates the skin. Certain medications and menopause, can really dry out the skin. Surface dehydration is usually due to using drying products, environmental factors, as well as hot showers. Many people tend to use "acne" products when they don't have acne. A few pimples acne does not make! Get a professional analysis from a reputable esthetician to find out what kind of products you should be using.

Acne

There can be (and are) whole books written on acne. Acne in my opinion has many causes. Many more people have acne now, than in the past. I personally believe this is due to stress and diet. America's current diet is horrible and filled with chemicals, preservatives and hormones our bodies can't digest or excrete fast enough through our liver and kidney, so they come out on our skin. Most dermatologists have no idea how to treat acne without writing a quick prescription and giving very drying products. So yes, the acne might clear up, but the repercussions on the skin are just as bad. Many dermatologists tend to make the skin worse because they usually only specialize in diagnosing diseases and writing prescriptions! They can't be bothered with the daily care of the skin. Many times they'll give you the samples the cosmetic or pharmaceutical companies gave them and hope you don't return.

Acne clients need a gentle cleanser, alpha–hydroxy acid exfoliator (no scrubs), a light moisturizer and a sun block to prevent discoloration of the new skin formed from open sores. Baking soda and water mixed into a paste and put on the skin, can also be a good exfoliator. Leave it on for about ten minutes and rinse off. Acne people need to do an internal cleansing and start their whole body/skin over. Then, get on a good skin regimen and stick to it. Stop trying to get perfect skin with no pimples, while jumping from product to product. It's better to stick to what may be more expensive products that work, than loads of cheaper ones that don't work. Regular facials will really help this population, in order to keep up with the changing needs of their skin. Remember not to pop a pimple unless it's ready! If you press on a pimple more than two or three times and nothing comes out, then leave it! That's how you scar. Don't use your nails either.

Fine Lines

Lines can be annoying and not very attractive. You usually can't get rid of lines from creams or magic! Aside from plastic surgery, here are a few things you can do to help minimize lines. Drink your sixty ounces of water a day. Don't use drying products on your skin. Pure vitamin C serums are great antioxidants that help prevent new lines from forming. Products with hylauronic acid are great because they hold a thousand times their weight in water and plump up the fine lines. I love pure meadowfoam serums. Exfoliate on a regular basis to get rid of dead, dry skin. This will prevent makeup from creasing in the lines. Peels, laser, and microdermabrasion will help to smooth the skin. Makeup is also another compliment to use as an illusion to minimize lines. This can be tricky if you don't know what you're doing. Some creams may look and feel like they make your wrinkles go away. They are just temporarily filling them in with potentially pore clogging ingredients. Pick your poison I guess. Beware of having pimples in your lines and then what? Sun block is the only answer to preventing most lines. Start young and never stop.

Dry Skin

Dry skin is skin that may be lacking oil. Many of us have dry skin all over our face and body or in certain parts of our face. Dry skin is not the same as skin that is lacking water. That is dehydrated skin. Dry skin can be due to genetics, taking hot showers, or using drying products. Menopause causes very dry skin. Although creams are a good fix for this, they only really, help if the other causes are fixed. A proper diet can help dry skin. Drink enough water and eating things like salmon and mackerel can help. Get enough omega oils. Hard water also contributes to dry skin. Just try living in New Jersey where we get clumps of minerals out of the tap!

Blackheads

A blackhead is caused by oil, dead skin cells, pollution and residue that build up in the pore. When it comes to the surface, it oxidizes, and turns black. Thus the name blackhead! Blackheads are fun! Some pores are just prone to blackheads and they will always need the maintenance. Life could be worse. The only way to really remove them is through squeezing. A cream won't get rid of them. Strips won't get rid of them either. Strips might remove the top layer, but the rest of the pore is still clogged. Beware of ingredients that are pore cloggers.

Nut Scrubs = Squeaky Clean

Just say no! Squeaky clean only works on your kitchen floor, not your face. If you like that tight dry feeling after you wash your face, and scrub the crap out of it like it's your bathtub, you are totally destroying your skin. Pull a cotton ball apart and imagine that is what a harsh scrub does to your skin. The collagen fibers that keep our skin together are like cotton. The scrubs microscopically destroy our collagen and skin. Maybe use that scrub on your feet or bathtub scum and that's it. I bet it will even take the paint of your car.

Dull

Dull skin is usually due to lack of exfoliation. If the rest of you're skin care program is being done correctly, than exfoliate or increase your exfoliation intensity. I always prefer a chemical exfoliation to a mechanical one. That means, use an acid over a scrub. Acids can go further into the skin, but in a gentler manner. Drug store and department store AHA's are usually not effective and I really don't recommend using them. They do not have enough acid to work and drug/department stores are not allowed to sell AHA's with a low enough pH to keep the acid effective. I would only purchase a product sold in a spa or by a dermatologist for exfoliating.

Most Common Complaints About Makeup and How to Correct Them

Read the Ingredients

Don't always believe what the people behind the counter tell you. They know they could tell a woman almost anything and she would believe it. Customers usually never question the BS they're given and they want to believe the dream, as well as the hype. Don't be fooled.

Makeup Gets Caked In Lines

There are a few reasons this could happen. Everything starts with the skin, so make sure your skin is well hydrated. Exfoliation is very important to get rid of dead skin and minimize lines. Make sure you're not putting too much makeup on your skin. The third problem could be the texture of the product. The texture might not be right for your skin type. Concealers tend to be composed of mineral oil, which becomes greasy and sits in the lines as the days go on. Always try to find a mineral oil free product. Blot with a tissue during the day if you're oily. The success of true mineral makeup has forced many companies to reformulate their foundation and concealer to be less pore clogging.

It is still very important to read the ingredients. It may say mineral makeup, but still have other pore clogging ingredients that are cheap and used as fillers.

Color Correcting

This is a great trick professionals use to fix skin. Be sure to use very little of the color corrector under your concealer. Blending is the key as always! Use the tricks listed under the dark eye circle section.

Green cancels out red.

Yellow cancels out purple.

Orange cancels out blue.

Orange also cancels out dark spots on darker skin.

How to Have Flawless Foundation

When you want to know if a foundation matches, put a swipe of foundation from your lower cheek down to your neck. It should match closely and melt right into the skin. Sometimes it helps to put a few swipes so you can see the difference in undertones and really know which one is best. I also like to check on my nose and cheek a bit, just to be sure. In the old days, foundations used to be very pink based. Now they make foundations more yellow/beige based, which tends to be more natural looking. No matter how natural looking the color, it will look unnatural, if it's the wrong color. Color selections can change as we age, and change from season to season as we tan. Watch for foundation powders that are talc based. These will clog pores. I recommend a mineral powder foundation if you have problems finding a talc free formula. It is harder for darker skins to do mineral foundations, because they turn ashy on dark skins. In all products, watch for mineral oil, isopropyl palmitate, lanolin, paraffin, and petrolatum, and isopropyl mystriate. These are also known pore cloggers.

Never try to make your skin more tan with foundation. Use a bronzer with a big brush for even application. Be careful putting shimmer bronzer all over your face. I recommend using a shimmer one on the body and a matte bronzer on the face. If you're oily, only use a little bit of bronzer over foundation that is half a shade lighter than your skin. As the day goes on, the oil from your skin will make your foundation and bronzer darker. Then you'll get that ugly "ring of fire", where you see the line of demarcation between your face and neck. Eww!

The Best Beauty Products

I feel like the Ralph Nader of the beauty industry. I have really high standards when it comes to beauty products. My clients will tell me if something doesn't work or if one product is a must have. I find that if I read the ingredients, I don't even have to try the product to know if it works. Of course, being a girl, I try it anyway! People always say, "If Lora says it works, it works." Since I live on a budget, I have not tried every product on the planet. From the products I have used, here are my favorites. As I try more, they will be listed on my blog and upcoming books. If you have any favorites please let me know and I'll try them out.

Foundation

M.A.C.
www.maccosmetics.com
I like Studio Fix or Studio Tech especially for darker skin tones. The Studio Fix has talc, which clogs pores, but gives great coverage. They have the absolute best color matching for darker skins, talc and all. You must use the #190 brush for the Studio Tech or else you'll use one compact per month.

Jane Iredale
www.janeiredale.com

The mineral foundation powder is great for light to medium skin tones. They press it into a compact for easy carrying.

Giorgio Armani
www.giorgioarmanibeauty–usa.com
I went to the Armani counter to try the Luminous Silk Foundation to see if all the hype was true. Hell yeah, I bought it after she did only one side of my face. I didn't even need concealer. I need so little to get great skin that it's so worth the price. Go paesano!

Mascara

M.A.C.
www.maccosmetics.com
Prolash black mascara is great. I'm a mascara girl, so I love it. I only use black mascara. Brown mascara is for pussies. If you're a blonde and think you really can't handle black mascara, use dark navy instead. This will make the eye pop more than brown. Let's be real, if brown mascara looked good, all fair colored celebrities would be wearing it, but they don't.

Maybelline
www.maybelline.com
I absolutely love the Define–A–Lash. The rubber tipped prongs make it so easy to literally "define a lash." Once you get used to working with the brush, you'll realize how great it is and how easy it is to get a good coating with one swipe. I love mascara so I like to go over the lashes a few times. With this brush you can do many passes without clumping.

Christian Dior
www.dior.com
Like everyone else I do love the Show mascara. The brush is really big and round and a bit difficult to use. It takes a while to get the hang of it. At first I didn't notice a difference to warrant the price, but I have to admit I get compliments on my lashes whenever I use it. I like compliments so every so often I splurge.

Brushes

M.A.C.
www.maccosmetics.com
I love M.A.C. Brushes and these are the highlights. I have used other brushes but I haven't found any that are that much better to warrant paying more than M.A.C. prices.

- The #150 is a big powder foundation brush and gives even coverage.
- The #226 is great for lining the eye. I also use it for eyebrows.
- The #190 brush for the Studio Tech is a must for a flawless application for other liquid foundations as well.

Anastasia of Beverly Hills
www.anastasia.net
I love the Duo brushes. They're great for applying powder to the eyebrows with the angled one end and then blending the powder with the wand on the other end. Genius.

Eye Shadows

M.A.C.
www.maccosmetics.com
I love the paints for an all day eye shadow base. This stuff is amazing. Use the neutral color under any shadow color or a colored paint under a similar color. I also like to mix them up to make a more bland color a bit more intense. You can of course use them alone with no shadow over them for a long lasting look. The traditional eye shadows are great and come in so many colors. I always believe in using some kind of shadow base to prolong color adhesion.

Urban decay
www.urbandecay.com
Their eye shadows are great and fabulous for glitter stuff.

NARS

www.narscosmetics.com

Their shadows are heavily pigmented which I love and I feel heavily pigmented products are always worth the price because you don't have to cram your brush in the shadow to get the color you want.

Eye Liners

Urban decay

www.urbandecay.com

Their 24/7 pencils don't last 24/7 but they last long and I love the great wild colors.

Xtreme Lashes

www.xtremelashes.com

Their Glideliners are *amazing*. They are waterproof and I have never used a liner that lasts that long. They are soft and so easy to apply its amazing. This is my number one eye pencil. They're not cheap but worth every damn penny. Put it on once and no need to reapply so it probably comes out cheaper than reapplying a cheaper liner.

Blinc

www.blincinc.com

These liquid eyeliners are awesome. The brush is very thin, easy to use and you only need to apply it once.

MAC

www.maccosmetics.com

These Liquilast liners really don't come off and you better know what you're doing and don't make any mistakes. I love the wild colors and they're great to use as eye shadow if you can maneuver it around above your other eyeliner. You might want to purchase a very thin brush instead of using the one they give you.

Lipgloss

Laura Mercier
www.lauramercier.com
I like her lip–gloss. The ones in tubes are my favorite. They're not tacky and gooey.

Concealer

Laura Mercier
www.lauramercier.com
The Secret Camouflage is amazing. It comes in a compact and you can either blend the colors together or use them alone. They are slightly dry so you need to sometimes blend with eye cream or moisturizer.

M.A.C.
www.maccosmetics.com
I like the Studio Finish concealer. They are also a bit drier and longer lasting.

Airbrush Makeup

Temptu
www.temptu.com
This is the professional industry standard. You can't beat airbrush for pretty much anything in terms of makeup.

Stream Cosmetics
www.streamcosmetics.com/lora
This would be considered the laymen's airbrush system. It is very easy to use with three pressure settings so you don't have to know the p.s.i. needed like professionals do. There is a ton of education provided to the consumer, which includes a DVD, online tutorials and distributors who will come to your house to help you. Yes, this is a company that has distributors and I loved the product so much, I became a distributor. They also have personal airbrush tanning systems that give the most

beautiful color. You know of course there is a special gift if you become a distributor under my name!

Mattify

Dr. Brandt No More Pores
www.drbrandtskincare.com
This product is amazingly good! I put it on my t–zone right before my foundation, and I stay matte all day long. I was really shocked. There might be some talc hidden in it, but sometimes a girl just wants to be matte!

Dermalogica
www.dermalogica.com
The Clearing Mattifier smoothes the skin texture and helps the clear the skin as well. If it stands up to New Jersey humid summers, it's a keeper.

Eyebrows

Anastasia of Beverly Hills
www.anastasia.net
Any of the eyebrow products by her are great. If you find some of the powders too ashy, try the pencil form or mix the powder with the wax for a finer line and a more pigmented color. Practice using the stencils and they'll become your best friend if you need to fill in or tweeze.

Maybelliene Define–A–Brow
www.maybelline.com
I really like these twist–up pencils. Twist–ups are great for your purse for obvious reasons. I like the colors and they're pretty easy to figure out.

Bronzer

MAC
www.maccosmetics.com

All the colors are good assuming you get the right shade for your skin color and don't over use it. If you're very oily, I recommend the matte on your face and the shimmer on your body. If you have very uneven texture, go easy on the bronzer and stick to matte.

Bobbi Brown
www.bobbibrowncosmetics.com
I really like her bronzer because there is no orange in it. It's matte and more on the brown side.

Physicians Formula
www.physiciansformula.com
I love their multi–color bronzer. I tend to use this on men because it's not so heavily pigmented which means it gives color without making any mistakes or making them look like they have bronzer on. Many times on set, you have to work fast and there is little time for blending so this works perfect.

Body Color

Scott Barnes Body Bling
www.scottbarnes.com
This is the only product I have found in the category that I love. This is basically what gives JLO her glow. It is a tinted, shimmering moisturizer. You really need to rub this cream in carefully in order to get thorough coverage. I also like to mix the light and dark together to create a medium tone. It's perfect when you need an instant tan or to cover sloppy self–tanning.

Tweezers

Anastasia of Beverly Hills
www.anastasia.net

Her tweezers are the best and I've used many different brands. I wonder if she can get different style tips with the same tension. It's the tension in her tweezers that set them apart from the rest. Even men love these and notice the difference.

Toothpaste

Umbrian Clay Toothpaste by Fresh
www.fresh.com

This is by far the best toothpaste in the world. No sugar or bad aftertaste. No foaming at the mouth like Cujo. Feel free to have this product shipped right to my house if you love me! This works great on pimples as well. Because there is no foaming, you can use this product dry on your finger to freshen breath. I put it on my tongue and move it all around after lunch if I don't have time to brush. Easy to keep in your purse or briefcase when you can't chew gum or suck on mint in the business environment.

Moisturizer

Crème Ancienne by Fresh
www.fresh.com

Yes, it really is worth the money. You can throw away all your other moisturizers besides sun block and just use this. Essentially you'll save money because you use very little and don't need to have separate eye, neck, throat, and face creams. It's great on lips, cuts, cuticles, and feet. My friend uses it on her eyelashes and then just curls them. It looks amazing. It's for dry skin. If you're oily, I would recommend just using this at night and sun block in the daytime.

Dermalogica
www.dermalogica.com

Any moisturizer by Dermalogica is great. I really love this line. My favorites are the Power Rich, Super Rich, Active Moist and Dynamic Skin Recovery.

Medicine of the People
www.medicineofthepeople.net
Pretty much any cream, moisturizer, salve by them is incredible. I found this company in Arizona and she actually uses Navajo recipes, which I swear are magical.

Serums & Oils

My sister makes the Phoenix Rising products and that's why I have it listed as the best in many categories. I think they're the best or else she wouldn't make them! She wanted to develop products that *we* would want to buy and use. Of course I have also included other product lines that I love to use in order to be fair.

Body Scrubs and Creams

Phoenix Rising Tropical Plantation Coffee Body Scrub
www.phoenixrisingskincare.com
Yummy, need I say more? If you really love your girlfriend or wife, I suggest you scrub her down with this before she showers. It's a great way to wake up. The pure coffee grinds smell amazing and really awakens the senses.

Light Hand Balm by Phoenix Rising
www.phoenixrisingskincare.com
Smells great and really works to heal the hands and dryness. I also put this on my lips for a quick fix. Men like this because it is not greasy and melts right into the skin.

Crack Spackle by Phoenix Rising
www.phoenixrisingskincare.com

Use this balm to fill in deep, painful cracks. This is perfect for men and those that work with their hands. It is also great for the deep cracks in the heels and bad cuticle rips. It also works amazing on diaper rash, florist hands, nurses and teachers.

Phoenix Rising Repairing Serum
www.phoenixrisingskincare.com
This is very similar to the Fresh Crème Ancienne serum, but cheaper and actually more pure. I love the rose essential oil in here as well. It's extremely repairing to the eye area. If you have dry or aging skin, this is a must.

Vitamin C Serums by Skin Ceuticals
www.skinceuticals.com
In my opinion, this is one of the best Vitamin C anti–aging serums. Splurge and get the highest percentage of Vitamin C since we only get one skin baby!

Nelly de Vuyst Oils
www.nellydevuyst.com
They are all great and very effective. I have had the St. Johns Wort for years. The borage oil is one of the best anti–wrinkle treatments out there. Their serums are some of the best on the market.

Young Living Oils
www.youngliving.com
There are not enough words to tell how much I love these oils. I swear I can feel my body heal when I use good essential oils. These are a big hit with my clients. The raindrop kit is a must have for preventing back problems, sickness and over all health. I use tea tree on pimples and ingrown hairs; lavender on cuts and peppermint for headaches and sore muscles.

Lip Balm

Fresh
www.fresh.com

I love the Sugar Lip Balm. It really is hydrating, tastes good and works. It's expensive but worth a splurge once in a while.

Phoenix Rising All Natural Skin Care
www.phoenixrisingskincare.com
I'm a girl so of course I love the Chocolate Lip Balms. The brown chocolate has a natural brown tint and the white chocolate is clear. So yummy and a great no calorie chocolate sugar fix. It's like I say, "Put it on your lips, not your hips."

Dermalogica
www.dermalogica.com
They have a lip treatment that is amazing. It's not really a lip balm, but more of a treatment. This is great for smokers and those with fine lines around the lips. It has a berry taste like Fruit Loops!

Aveda
www.aveda.com
I really like the Lip Saver. It is a heavy almost waxy type consistency. I like it when it feels like my lips need something to really protect them and put an occlusive layer over my lips.

Peppermint Lip Balm by Medicine of the People
www.medicineofthepeople.net
The Peppermint Balm in the tin is convenient and contains Hisiiyaanii to get rid of cold sores naturally.

Fragrance

This is a very personal category and you'll either like it or not. I'm just going to list my favorite perfumes. I like men's cologne since I like musky, sandalwood smells. I love anything that smells like Catholic Church! I also tend to mix my perfumes together to get the better of each one.

Gucci
www.gucci.com

The only one I absolutely love from them is the men's Pour Homme. This is Catholic Church in a bottle. It has white pepper, ginger, papyrus wood, amber and leather. It also reminds me of an incredibly sexy, long lost love who broke my heart.

Fresh
www.fresh.com
Sake fragrance is so captivating. Ginger, white peach and sandalwood make this light with many layers. The Fig Apricot is the most amazing blend and I actually use this as my bathroom spray because it is so relaxing. Who knew green tea and petit grain could smell so good.

Stila
www.stilacosmetics.com
I love the Crème Bouquet. It is a very vanilla smell but the pink lilac and lily of the valley make it not so nauseatingly sweet.

Christian Dior
www.dior.com
Hypnotic Poison is another vanilla fragrance without being nauseatingly sweet. It's a bit heavier than Crème Bouquet. It has bitter almond, Sambac jasmine and vanilla musk. The body lotion is also nice and doesn't have that funky smell that many matching perfume lotions have.

Candles

Fresh
www.fresh.com
Most if not all the candles from Fresh are amazing. Here are a few of my favorites:

- Demitasse – coffee in a candle
- Sake – sniffing might cause intoxication
- Rose – more real than roses

Diptyque
www.diptyqueparis.com
I like their candles but the one I love the most is Essence of John Galliano. Leave it to me to like the most expensive one! It smells like birch wood embers, iris and vanilla musk.

Face Cleaner and Exfoliaters

Lora's Favorite Cleanser is of course named after me! This cleanser might feel different at first but once you get used to the oatmeal consistency you'll appreciate just how well it cleans your skin without stripping. It has crushed fresh lavender and the smell is out of this world.

Phoenix Rising
www.phoenixrisingskincare.com
The Brown Rice Cleanser is great for oily/congested skin. It's also good for normal to dry skin that once in a while feels grimy. Gentle, but amazingly makes your skin feel so clean without drying.

Nelly De Vuyst
www.nellydevuyst.com
The Cellular Matrix cleanser is a milky cleanser that is great for dry and normal skin. It just feels so rich and luxurious.

Dermalogica
www.dermalogica.com
The Special Cleansing Gel is great for normal to oily skin. Even acne can use this since it will clean but not strip or irritate sensitive skin.

Makeup Remover

Phoenix Rising
www.phoenixrisingskincare.com
This make–up remover is drag queen tested and approved! It really melts the makeup and acts like an eye treatment as well. Try the rose based one to heal the fine lines around the eye area.

Xtreme
www.xtremelashes.com
Their make–up remover is 100% oil free. By FDA laws, products only need to be 70% oil free in order to be listed as oil free. It is more difficult for a 100% oil free make-up remover to work because oil dissolves oil If you have eyelash extensions, this is the must have makeup remover for eyelash extensions.

Shaving Oils and Creams

Phoenix Rising
www.phoenixrisingskincare.com
This is a tough one for men to deal with, but once they get used to it, they love it. Put a very thin layer of oil on and then your shaving cream over it if you like. Shave away, but remember to rinse the razor after each pass. The result is baby smooth skin. This can be used for women as well, and all that is needed is a thin layer for shaving.

Fresh
www.fresh.com
Their shaving cream is really smoothing and comforting to the skin. Olive oil and meadowfoam make this very gentle on the skin.

Dermalogica
www.dermalogica.com
They also have shaving oil that is very nice.

Sunscreens

Skin Ceuticals Sunblock
www.skinceuticals.com
They're all great. I have my clients use the sunscreen as their day cream. I recommend a serum if you need more hydration. Moisturizers with sunscreen are not very effective so just use one product to do the job.

Dermalogica
www.dermalogica.com
I also recommend all of the dermalogica sun products. I really like the stick and spray. As always make sure you apply it generously.

Shower Cleansers

Fresh
www.fresh.com
Fig Apricot
I love this smell. Men would definitely like this. It's more musky than flowery.
Milk Milk Shower Gel
It is baby fresh, clean and soft. Pay a few bucks extra for the pump. Something about the smell of this reminds me of when I was a kid.

Laura Mercier
www.lauramercier.com
I love her shower gels and body creams. All the body products smell great and feel good. The Coconut Body Butter and the Chocolate Truffle Body Bath are divine.

Haircare

Fresh
www.fresh.com
Meadowfoam Hair Conditioner – What a blessed salvation for fried hair. Great for any kind of hair that needs conditioning. It doesn't make your hair limp even if your hair is fine.

Lora Condon

Teeth Whitening

Whiter Image
www.whiterimage.com
They have great in-salon teeth whitening where you get about 6 shades whiter in 45 minutes. You won't get fluorescent white which looks really strange, just pearly white. You can also do it in fifteen minute intervals which is great for those short on time, money or pain tolerance.

The Best Spa Services

Hot Stone Massage – The hot stones melt the muscles, to further loosen muscle tissue and further relaxation. This massage is only good if you have a good therapist. It's more annoying than restful if the therapist is not well versed in this technique.

Thai Massage – It feels great to be stretched by someone else. You feel like you're working out and a foot taller afterwards. You wear loose fitting clothes for this treatment. It's also called yoga for the lazy.

Pumpkin Peel Facial – It burns at first, but that's just the pumpkin enzyme eating the dead skin cells. Extractions are so easy to do on clients after this treatment. Your skin will feel plumped up, soft and smooth afterwards unlike some straight glycolic peels.

Sake Body Treatment – You'll find this at Fresh spa, unless you can find someone else who does it like they do. Mi–so relaxed!

Brown Sugar Body Polish – This is also at Fresh spa. Your skin will be creamier than butter after this. Parkay!

Raindrop Therapy – It's an amazing essential oil treatment, where oils are placed down your spine, and on your feet to purify the blood. The oils actually stay in your system for a week. Many people have great healing stories from this treatment. I highly recommend this for those with an immune system that is constantly under attack. This would include flight attendants, teachers, medical professionals and those under constant stress. Ok, that probably includes everyone! I would recommend actually just buying Young Living Oils and doing this at home on yourself or have someone do this to you. The quality of the oil is of the utmost importance, because of the molecular action of pure oils, as opposed to those with impurities. It's kind of like homemade tacos vs. Taco Bell. I happen to love Taco Bell, but it's not where I would derive quality nutrients.

Reiki – This is a Japanese based energy balancing and healing. I'm a reiki master; so of course, I'm partial to the effects of reiki. Everyone loved Mr. Miagi and how he healed Daniel! Well he was doing reiki! Typically, you lay down clothed and the therapist lays their hands on different parts of your body. This is not massage. You might feel heat from their hands and some tingling. Reiki can also be done from a distance since we all know energy travels!

Reflexology – It will feel like a foot massage to you, but a good therapist, can rub on different pressure points of the feet to clean out the body, or find potential health problems. Make sure you drink a lot of water after this treatment to flush out the toxins. If you don't, you might get sick or a headache. It can hurt, but that usually means you have something going on in that part of the foot or corresponding organ.

Steam Shower – There is nothing better after a massage. It's worth the extra few dollars some spas charge.

IPL Photofacial – Sometimes you can't beat technology for anti–aging, spot removal and broken capillaries. Intense Pulsed Light is very different and much more effective than traditional laser so please don't let a traditional laser people tell you that your light hair can't be treated.

Oxygen Facial – One of the coolest facials I have ever given and received. It just makes the skin look radiant and oh so clean. You skin will be a shade lighter after this treatment.

Nelly de Vuyst Oxygen Facial – This is amazing. A foam mask is placed over different oils and creams. When the bubbles of the foam break, it causes an oxygen chemical reaction that forces the oils to penetrate into the skin. It feels like Rice Crispies on your face as the foam bubbles burst. The result is glowing, ultra hydrated skin.

Biofeedback – This is very noninvasive, yet extremely effective. It clears the energy pathways using electrical current, acupressure and flower essences to bring the body system back into balance; expensive but worth every penny.

The Best Therapists, Artists, and Organizations

Jason Hayes
www.jasonhayesnyc.com
He is the most fabulous hair and makeup artist ever. He has the best stories. My hero! He keeps getting more and more talented. He's a true renaissance man and has worked with Nicole Kidman, Uma Thurman and RuPaul, need I say more? If you get the chance to have him work on you, bring him a good bottle of red wine.

Tobi Britton
www.themakeupshop.com
She is a very creative hair and makeup artist located in New York. She is a great makeup teacher and I still hear her advice in my head.

Florin Badea
www.badeaandsoul.com
I highly recommend him for any type of massage or healing. He is one of the best in the world. Limit him to only one Long Island ice tea! I nicknamed him the Romanian Crush, knots don't stand a chance against him! He has an A–List clientele, but remains extremely humble. He's a true example of the American Dream. You can find his healing hands at the Badea and Soul Holistic Center in Hotel Fauchere in Milford, Pennsylvania.

Mezzaluna Spa
www.mezzalunadayspa.com

Great stone massages and extremely well versed in different massage techniques located in Westwood, New Jersey.

Fresh Espace in NYC
www.fresh.com

This is the perfect for the service redeemable in product. There are no extractions in the facials, so I would get the body treatment.

Anastasia of Beverly Hills
www.anastasia.net

Yup, she's one of the best in brows. I was one of her East Coast trainers and that training was priceless. She is grace under fire and I would love to be her friend.

William Pfaltz

He is the guru of biofeedback. His incredible passion is almost as powerful as the computer and machines he uses for biofeedback. His company is the House of Wellness in Millburn, New Jersey.

Jack Canfield
www.jackcanfield.com

Jack is like the wise, loving grandfather that we all wished we had. Kind of like a spiritual Santa. His book, *The Success Principles* is awesome and I recommend anyone who wants to have a smidgen of success read this book. It's a great gift for grads assuming they read it. On his website, he gives a free ninety day success goal chart. I use it and find it helps to keep me on track with my loads of goals. I went to his one–day success seminar and it was awesome. I highly recommend going. He stayed until every book was signed and pictures were taken.

Peak Potentials and T. Harv Eker
www.peakpotentials.com

There is not enough I can say for Harv and his company. I got a free ticket to the Millionaire Mind Seminar after I bought his book. The first day I didn't love it at all but something told me to stay and finish the three days. The second day was really great and the third day was amazing. I couldn't believe how much information we were given for a free three–day seminar. The free seminar was so great I eventually signed up for the Enlightened Warrior Training and again it was one of the most incredible experiences of my life. The year after, I went to the Wizard Training Camp and again I had the most incredible experience and was in awe of what I learned, felt, changed, released and produced. I made friends for life while changing my life. If you've been to any of the classes, you know what I'm talking about.

The Secret
www.thesecret.tv
Well if you haven't heard about the movie, The Secret, then get out from under the rock you've been living under and go on their site and watch the movie for a few bucks. This was really life changing for me since I thought the complete opposite before seeing the movie.

Bob Proctor
www.bobproctor.com
His books and teachings started the major changes in my life. He's no–nonsense and his manner of speaking reminds me of Ross Perot. Straight shooting logic that really gets my lazy butt off the couch and working towards achieving my goals.

Ricky's
www.rickysnyc.com
This is one of my favorite places to go in New York. It's like Sephora and Spencers mixed together. They have all types of beauty products, makeup, wigs, Halloween costumes and sex toys. It's all so random. Tons of very cool stuff all geared towards making you look beautiful or at least laughing your ass off. Welcome to New York!

The Best Health Items

Loose Green Teas
Matcha green tea powder is amazing and the health benefits are endless.
I get mine from the Green Tea Terrace in California. If you live by an
Asian area definitely try those markets and try some new teas.

Loose Earl Grey Tea
Bergamont oil, which is found in earl grey tea, is used as an anti–
depressant. I make mine with milk and sugar. It's a great way to wean
off of coffee.

Peppermint Oil
Amazing for headaches, stress or stomachache and back problems.

Medicinal Teas
Echinacea, ginkgo, rice and of course green.

Heated Herbal Pack
You know those things you get in the mall kiosk? You put them in the
microwave and place them on muscles or your stomach for PMS. Many
nights this thing saved my back.

Magboys
Magnet rollerballs to ease pain in my wrists and joints. Good magnets
are great items overall and I love them

Sore No More
Kind of like bengay or biofreeze, but I like this more since its pepper based. Oye caliente!

Kevin Trudeau
"Natural Cures They Don't Want You To Know About"
I have the book and newsletters. It's hard to follow all of his rules. Sometimes a girl just wants a taylor ham, egg and cheese on a bagel. His info is right on target and gets you thinking about how fragile our bodies are and how the food industry really screws us.

Dr. Weil
Any book by him is amazing, just good old fashion eating. The way we're supposed to eat and live.

The Prescription for Nutritional Healing
Required reading for everyone. You'll be amazed how often you'll end up referring to it.

Howard Stern Private Parts and Miss America
Everyone needs a good laugh to reduce stress. The chapter on Michael Jackson was one of the funniest things I have ever read. Laughing keeps you young and healthy. Hey now!

The Master Cleanser
I love this drink, even if I'm not able to stop eating for 40 days!

More Stories From Other Spa Workers

I asked some of my friends for a few of their stories. Here are some that kept me laughing for months and years afterward. I also added a few more of my own. I hope you enjoy them as much as I did. Please send me some of your stories for the next book!

Clarence Thomas Lives –
One of my friends was working in a spa and banging one of her coworkers. What better way to end a hard day, then getting busy in the spa room on a nice heated bed. They ended many hard days with many hard nights. The morning after one of their encounters, one of her coworkers called her in and showed her what she uncovered. It was pubic hair on the sheets! What if a client found it before she did? That's disgusting! Obviously, she knew they were getting busy the night before and everything comes out in the wash! The lesson is, just change the sheets afterwards. I still wonder whose hair it actually was!

Safe Spa
I guess there is a theme going on here, but yes, it's another sex in the treatment room story. One day an esthetician found used condoms on the floor of her treatment room. When she left the spa, the night before, she locked the doors. Someone who had the key went into the spa and had sex in one of the treatment rooms. The next day, the esthetician told the manager, and the manager got all crazy and blamed one of the

massage therapists. None of the massage therapists had a key to the spa. Only the manager did! That eliminated everyone else besides the manager. Apparently, she went out after work, got drunk and brought some guy back to the spa. She was known for doing this and finally got caught. At least we worked in a "safe spa."

Got Milk?

My one friend was doing a makeup application on a woman who was carrying her toddler around. The toddler was crying and she couldn't get the kid to stop. The client whipped out her boob, and had her toddler suck on her breast. She told the makeup artist to keep doing her makeup because she planned on buying some new makeup. The makeup artist got really grossed out, because the woman didn't even have milk in her breasts. She was just using her boob as a pacifier! I swear I'm not making this stuff up!

Lockdown

Right before I started working in one salon, the manager who was a bit psycho (surprise, surprise), had a harder day than usual. Her staff was giving her a hard day and she got so frazzled, she actually locked herself in the bathroom. This was the only bathroom in the spa. She wouldn't come out, even though the customers needed to use the restroom. The staff kept asking her to come out and she wouldn't. A half hour went by, and they finally called her boyfriend of eight years to come and get her out. He actually had to leave work and come down to the spa to talk his girlfriend out of the bathroom. It was a small town and people loved to talk. This is a story that lives on in infamy! The manager thought she was still a ballerina and always talked about ballet, even though she hadn't danced since she was a little girl. I mean she wore the tight bun and walked like she had a broomstick up her ass, yet she hadn't danced in years.

Happy Endings

One day I was listening to Howard Stern, and Chaunce Hayden, the owner of Steppin' Out Magazine, was telling Howard that his usual massage therapist, all of the sudden started to give him happy endings. This freaked me out for two reasons:

1. Not long before, I met Chaunce at a photo shoot I did in his house with Justine Priestley. He seemed like an average, normal, professional guy.
2. I knew that Chaunce went to the spa I was working in at the time and got massages there. I was horrified, and couldn't picture any of our therapists doing this nastiness!

I had no idea how to approach the owner, and if I even should. Was it my business and moral obligation to tell her? Personally, I felt like it was, due to the fact that it would give us a bad reputation. Any men coming into the spa in the future might get the same idea! As soon as I got to work, I approached the owner and shyly said, "I heard Chaunce mention on Howard Stern this morning that his massage therapist gives him happy endings and I know he comes here!" She laughed, and said, "It was a different massage therapist that he goes to and she doesn't work at this spa." I was so relieved. We had a good laugh and went on with our day.

I was doing the makeup for a T.V. show featuring Stacey London and Phillip Bloch. I did Stacey's makeup no problem. I was really afraid of her because she gave me all her colors and told me exactly where to put them and how she wanted to look. When there is no creative license, it can be scary for an artist because we now have to exactly match the idea in person's head. It went well; no complaints and she even complimented my seven dollar J.C. Penny necklace. I then started on Phillip and men are usually pretty easy. After doing his makeup, he asked me for a cuticle cutter. I didn't have one and he just looked at me with disgust, put his hand up in the air and said, "Oh, you're not a real makeup artist." He then slithered out of the chair and walked away.

Final Words for Now!

If you read this far in the book, I hope you enjoyed my roller coaster of a life! I absolutely love what I do, and I love learning new techniques and keeping up on the latest trends. I can't imagine doing anything else or having to work in an office. I'm sure my past office employers would agree! I hope this book shows you that we are all really the same and our differences are what keep life interesting. We all have insecurities, strengths and weaknesses. Go with your gut and feel comfortable in your own skin, pimples and all!

Please email me your stories and questions about the beauty industry. I would love to publish them in my next book. Also, you can come to see me in my little corner of the world at Magic Hands Skin and Body Care in my hometown of Springfield, NJ. Magic Hands also has a Facebook where you'll find updates.

We all have a great story to tell! My websites are www. MakeUpWithMe.com and www.thelashdr.com. Please come and see me or at least email me your stories. If you bring in your book, you'll get 50% off any treatment. If you can't get to the salon, email me your receipt for the purchase of this book and you'll get a certificate for a free distant reiki healing session.

You can also check out my blog at www.spawars.blogspot.com. Here you'll find updates on Spa Wars, appearances and new info on products, procedures and everything beauty.

I wish everyone peace and love. A–ho!

Lora Condon
Beauty Consumer Advocate

About the Author

Lora Condon has been a licensed esthetician since 1998. Her makeup and eyelash extensions have been seen all over the world including Burger King, Ladies Home Journal, ESPN, Good Morning America and The Olive Garden.

Lora is a beauty consumer advocate, spa consultant and motivational speaker. Stay updated at www.makeupwithme.com.